THE BUSY MANAGER'S GUIDE TO MARKETING

THE BUSY MANAGER'S GUIDE TO MARKETING

Bill Donaldson

(G) GOODFELLOW PUBLISHING

(G) Published by Goodfellow Publishers Limited,
Woodeaton, Oxford, OX3 9TJ
http://www.goodfellowpublishers.com

British Library Cataloguing in Publication Data: a catalogue record
for this title is available from the British Library.

Library of Congress Catalog Card Number: on file.

ISBN: 978-1-906884-06-2

Production: P.K. McBride

Printed by Lightning Source, www.lightningsource.com

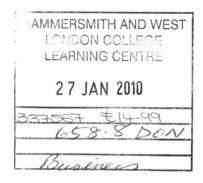

CONTENTS

LIST OF FIGURES

LIST OF TABLES

REFERENCES

Alderson, Q. (1957) *Marketing Behavior and Executive Action* Homewood, Ill.

Irwin Ansoff, I. (1987) *Corporate Strategy* London: Pelican Books

Boston Consulting Group (1977) as Hedley, B. Strategy and the Business Portfolio *Long Range Planning* February, Vol. 10, 1, pp 9–15

Maslow, A. H. (1970) *Motivation and Personality*, 2nd edition, New York: Harper Row

Kotler, P. (1997) *Marketing Management: Analysis, Planning Implementation and Control*, 9th edition, Englewood Cliffs,

Kotler, P. (2003) *Marketing Management: Millennium Edition*, Pearson

Kotler, P. and Keller, K. L. (2006) *Marketing Management*, 12th edition, Upper Saddle River, N.J.: Pearson

Piercy, N. (1991) *Market-Led Strategic Change* London: Harper Collins

ABOUT THE AUTHOR

Bill Donaldson is Professor of Marketing at The Robert Gordon University and is responsible for research in Marketing within the Aberdeen Business School. After more than a decade in sales and marketing positions Bill joined the University of Strathclyde as a lecturer in 1983 and obtained his doctorate in Industrial Marketing a decade later.

Author of *Sales Management: Principles, Process and Practice* (3rd edn, Palgrave, 2007), and *Strategic Market Relationships* (2nd edn, Wiley, 2007 with Tom O'Toole) his research interests continue in the area of sales management and relationship marketing. Bill has taught marketing at undergraduate, postgraduate and extensively on MBA programmes both at home and overseas.

ACKNOWLEDGEMENTS

The author wishes to thank Gerald Michaluk, Marketing Management Services International, for working on an earlier draft of this book and allowing much of his material to be used in this edition. Also, Colin Wheeler, Professor of Marketing at the University of Portsmouth, for contributing material in Chapter 6. Thanks to these two good friends.

The author and publishers wish to thank the following for permission to use copyright material:

Pearson Education for Table 2.3 'The Competitive Advantage Selection' from Kotler, 2003, p 313 (Table 11.2); Figure 4.2 'The Augmented Product' from Kotler, 2003, p 408 (Figure 14.2) and Figure 2.7 'The Marketing Information System' from Kotler, 1997, p 111 (Figure 4.1).

Harper Row for Figure 2.3 'Maslow's Hierarchy of Needs' from Maslow, A. H. (1970) *Motivation and Personality* 2nd edition, New York: Harper Row, p 00.

European Marketing Pocket Book 2000 (Henley-on-Thames) p 10 for Figure 3.3 'Europe's Changing Population'.

Elsevier Science Ltd for Figure 2.6 the Boston Box from *Long Range Planning* February, 1977, Vol 10, 1, pp 9–15.

FOREWORD

Bill Donaldson has put together a very informative guide to marketing – a subject which, in our modern competitive environment, no manager can afford to ignore.

There is no business that is exempt from competition and there are very few customers whose loyalty will survive more than one bad experience. However, those customers who experience satisfaction at all levels can become customers for life.

Marketing is not the sole preserve of the Marketing Director and his/her team: every member of staff from the receptionist and telephonist to the operators and technicians needs to be wise to the customer' needs, to the competition and to the market in which the organisation operates. We must ensure that we take every step necessary to identify our customer's desires and deliver those to a standard acceptable to them.

Market awareness is also important in relationships to those within our organisations. We must meet the expectations of our people who produce and deliver the service or products. If we do not meet our own people's expectations, we cannot expect them to meet those of our customers, and we lose the loyalty of our external customers by failing to match up to expectations, so we will also lose the loyalty of our internal customers.

As Bill Donaldson says, today's domestic market is as much multi-cultural as is the international market. If we are to retain and increase our market penetration at home and abroad, we must present our products and services taking account of cultural sensitivities at home as much as we do for overseas markets. A high degree of emotional intelligence is a pre-requisite for modern management, particularly as expressed through our marketing efforts.

Marketing impinges on virtually every management consideration including:

- financial, economic and legal implications of the business's activities

- emotional and interactive relationships with customers, suppliers and staff, regulators, bankers and the general public and all areas of our communities
- design and quality of production
- all 'statements' made by the organisation

Enjoy and learn from this book.

Sir Tom Farmer CBE, KCSG

Maidencraig Investments, Edinburgh

1   THE CONCEPT OF MARKETING

Marketing is selling goods that don't come back, to people that do

Peter Drucker

INTRODUCTION

The theory and practice of marketing have been, for too long, the preserve of the academic world and those businesses, usually in consumer goods, large enough to have professional marketing staff within their organisation. As a result, much of the wealth of knowledge and practical experience of marketing is either not known, or ignored as not part of their concern, by a considerable number of small to medium-sized companies, oil service businesses and others. Yet, more than ever, the busy manager can benefit from the information and knowledge available to enhance their understanding of the subject and widen the opportunity for these companies to utilise marketing skills and procedures for their own benefit.

The academic and theoretical flavour to many of the books written on marketing are, of course, admirably suited for the full-time student or what would be called the professional marketer. This book is aimed more towards the entrepreneur or non-professional marketers, busy managers, who are seeking ways and means of improving their business by the employment of practical marketing measures. In recent years, the author's experience in giving marketing lectures to small and first-time business owners and managers has confirmed the belief that a need exists for some form of practical marketing guide, which captures the essential elements of marketing and translates them into measures which can support the undoubted ambitions of such people.

This book contains the major core issues of marketing in a concentrated format, which hopefully is easy to follow and digest. It traces the marketing process through a logical progression to the marketing plan. It emphasises the practical nature of its content by being concise and easy to read and refer to. A book of this size is not intended to include a mass of supporting detail so academic references have been kept to a minimum. Instead, it has focused on the most important factors and essential components of the marketing process to provide practical support to business efficiency. The general concepts presented here are not related to the size and nature of a business, or any experience level, and its contents should also appeal to the wider reaches of the marketing world. However, to make it relevant to particular types of business the text has been customised with a wealth of up-to-date information to help the reader operate and compete more effectively.

A word of warning may be appropriate at this point. Many people have preconceived ideas about marketing, favourable or otherwise, because we come into contact with marketing activities and practices every day of our lives. For this reason the subject is interesting and stimulating and, in general, is not hard to understand. For example, we see TV and newspaper advertisements or posters, we meet sales people and we all purchase a vast array of goods and services. Everyone may have an opinion on an advertisement – whether it is good or bad – but few really understand how the communication process works and what is effective and ineffective in advertising, how to decide how much to spend, which media to use and how to measure its effect. While exact answers may not be possible, it is hoped that by reading this book the reader will be more informed about marketing management and be able to use his or her assets, skills and scarce resources more effectively and efficiently.

THE CONCEPT OF MARKETING

Marketing is the means by which a business becomes successful and is a key factor in the exchange process of a product from source to end-user. Therefore the concept of marketing rests fairly and squarely on the needs and wants of the customer. Although there is no one accepted definition of marketing, and a variety to pick from, the most appropriate and concise definition is the one from the Chartered Institute of Marketing:

> 'Marketing is the management process responsible for identifying, anticipating and satisfying customer requirements profitably.'

It would be wrong to assume that marketing is limited simply to the exchange of products. The traditional boundaries of marketing have been extended to include the service sector, in which profit and non-profit organisations, such as banks, charities, universities and even governments, have turned to marketing to influence their target audience. In the context of this book the use of product is synonymous with the service sector.

In marketing the mantra of identifying and satisfying customers' needs profitably is sacrosanct, yet if business is about anything other than making money it is surely about identifying (or creating) opportunities and how to take advantage of them. The result of this is that, for most organisations, effectiveness in marketing should be based on a marketing process that is conducted from the perspective of the customer; and a closer examination of customers' needs and wants becomes necessary. Needs are few in number and represent the essentials for human living, e.g. food, clothing etc. Wants to fulfil these needs are many and based on human perceptions, desires, and extraneous pressures such as peer group, culture and social environment. These wants are transformed into requirements for products, when the individual is in a position and willing to buy them. The role of the marketer is to influence this demand. Put simply, a child may need shoes but want Nike Air trainers!

The position of marketing in relation to your business and your customers is a matter of organisational judgement and decision. Figure 1.1 shows two variations, the common factor being that each has the customer as the centre of focus.

The marketing concept rests on four main tenets: a well-defined market; a focus on customer needs; a co-ordination of market activities affecting customers; and profitability through customer satisfaction. The orientation of marketing on the customer is now the most important consideration in the concept and goes beyond customer satisfaction. Indeed, leading market-led and customer-driven organisations go so far as to say that their aim is to delight the customer and such an aim may hold the secret of these companies and their business success. In the West the customer is King but in Japan the customer is God. Those who aspire to such high standards of performance must remember that customers will expect these standards as a matter of routine, once they have been established.

Figure 1.1 Marketing's role in business

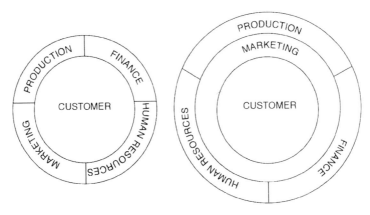

The concept is as much concerned with internal marketing as external marketing. It makes no sense to advertise the service your business can give before it is ready to provide quality service. Internal marketing should precede external marketing and ensure that able employees are successfully recruited, trained and motivated to serve customers to the standards you have set. Marketing is too important to be left to one person or a department; everyone in the company needs to focus on the value and satisfaction they provide for the customer, whether directly in contact with customers or indirectly in a support role. The abundance of choice available in the modern market place to satisfy customer needs enables customers to look for excellence in quality, value and cost. It is therefore not sufficient to be good at what you do; you must strive for excellence in the satisfaction of customer needs and wants, competitively and profitably. But be wary as raising expectations and failing to deliver can quickly result in customer dissatisfaction. Leading companies avoid this trap. As a senior IBM sales manager pointed out in a recent interview with the author:

> 'We consider it a sacking offence to promise a customer something you cannot deliver.'

Another aspect of the marketing concept is concerned with the ability of your business to react and adapt to the continuous change in the market place. To repeat, the necessity of identifying or creating opportunities and how you take advantage of them is at the heart of the marketing concept. You must develop the art of forward planning, which will mesh your business aims and resources with changing market opportunities. Marketing plays a major part in the process, analysing business situations, developing opportunities and defining plans to implement your business requirements.

Marketing, like many other specialist subjects, has its own descriptive terminology and it is appropriate at this stage to examine the main marketing terms, highlighted in bold below, that recur throughout the book. The most common terms are **strategies**, **goals** and **objectives** which form the basis of your planning effort. In essence, **strategy** makes it all happen. It is the 'game plan' of your marketing effort and is what your business is about, your vision of what it is you are trying to do and, in broad terms, how you intend to do it. **Goals** relate more to tactical operations and should be quite specific, singular and measurable. An **objective** is a measurable operational target such as achieving sales of £X value at Y% profit within a specified time period.

The nature of your **competition** is, of course, fundamentally important to the way you do business and will be examined in more detail later. It will remain a key issue throughout the marketing process and will never be absent from your planning considerations. The ability to identify the wants and needs of your existing and potential customers, match your operations to satisfying those needs better than the competition and delivering superior value is at the heart of a successful business. To do this there has to be a benefit, **a unique selling point or core benefit**, which allows your business to differentiate itself positively from competition and satisfy the needs of your customers. In other words, allow yourself time to think of the most favourable options to achieve your business aims.

The **utility, value and satisfaction** a consumer places on a product are characteristics of an alignment in which human needs are met by perceived benefits. The process a consumer goes through in making a decision is a target for both consumer and market research. It is of fundamental importance to a marketing plan in defining the perceptions, judgement, preferences and, finally, evaluation a consumer makes in the choice of a product. The variations are numerous and complex and representative of one of the more intangible core concepts of the marketing process.

Exchange has been defined as the act of obtaining a desired product from someone by offering something in return. As such it is one of the basics of marketing. If two parties are negotiating an exchange and reach an agreement, a transaction has taken place. A **transaction** formalises an exchange and is part of a larger aspect, that of **relationship marketing**, in which long-standing, trusting relationships are forged between customers and suppliers, by strengthening the ties between them. This will build a **marketing network**, which cuts costs, procedures and time in the negotiation of transactions as a matter of routine.

There are a number of subsidiary concepts which will be considered in more detail later in this book but are introduced as a guide to the direction in which the reader will eventually be be taken:

- Market segmentation – a market segment is a set of customers who have enough common characteristics and needs so that the same marketing methods can be used effectively to reach all of them.

- Market positioning – also called target marketing – is the approach taken in distinguishing your product or service from all other products by exploiting meaningful differences and distinctive competencies in the eyes of the customer.

- Market entry – your success or failure will also depend on the extent to which you are seen as credible. It is much easier for an established, known supplier than for a new entrant. The firm who no-one has heard of, whose products are untried and whose people are unknown will have a difficult task to make a sale and become established in the market.

- Marketing mix – the set of factors controlled by you and used to influence customers to purchase products. These factors or elements of the marketing mix (shown in Figure 1.2) do not always apply in every situation. The skill in marketing management is to use and manipulate these elements where they have greatest effect. By adding or subtracting or modifying products, by raising or lowering prices, by anticipating and cultivating different distribution methods and by your expenditure and effectiveness in selling, advertising and other promotional techniques, your firm can achieve market success and competitive advantage. This forms the marketing plan but requires information via research, customer feedback and auditing techniques on the effectiveness of previous marketing mix decisions.

Marketing maxims can be deceptively simple. You need a product which consumers want and can afford to buy, therefore your task is to improve production and distribution efficiency and bring down prices. You need quality products at reasonable prices thus reducing the costs of your promotional effort. Yet you need to stimulate demand by providing information and, sometimes, persuasion to buy; and you need to deliver customer satisfaction and, if possible, customer delight by superior service. Finally, you have to do this within legal and ethical boundaries so that you increase consumer and societal wellbeing at the same time as satisfying organisational goals and responsibilities.

Figure 1.2 The marketing mix

Elements	•	Market research
	•	Product planning
	•	Pricing
	•	Branding
	•	Packaging
	•	Channels of distribution
	•	Advertising, sales promotion
	•	Selling and merchandising
	•	Customer service

These concepts are illustrative in the sense that they are options which can be employed to suit your business, once you have thoroughly examined its capabilities and potential. The emphasis is on analysis and planning, to provide the key to the direction of your business and what you wish to achieve. The marketing management process provides the foundation for success in business.

2 THE MARKETING PROCESS

**Marketing is merely a civilised form of warfare, in
which most battles are won with words, ideas and
disciplined thinking**

Albert W Emery

THE PROCESS

The marketing process is continuous, analytical and progressive. It combines the strategy of long-term business
objectives with the tactics of short-term goals. It co-ordinates
the various sub-elements of marketing in mutual support of
business aims and maintains the focus on the customer. It
formulates from strategic planning the necessary marketing
action plans and carries them out. It provides an evaluation
and analysis of the different stages of business performance,
giving you the opportunity to adjust and change direction
where necessary.

Figure 2.1 The basic elements of marketing

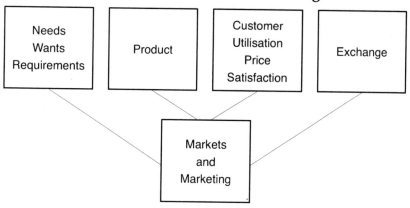

There are a number of basic factors and principles which require an understanding before we expand on them later in the book. The interlock between them is shown in Figure 2.1. Customer needs are influenced by a number of factors: political, economic, cultural, social, psychological and technological. An understanding of the interaction between them is necessary for marketing to be effective. It is also noteworthy at this stage to highlight the difference between the consumer and the customer. The consumer is the end-user of the product, who may or may not be the customer. The purchase of toothpaste for children is a good example, in which the mother is the customer and the children are the consumers. In pharmaceuticals the customer is the doctor or medical specifier whereas the patient is the consumer. As we shall see later in the book, in organisational buying, identifying customers, specifiers and users can become quite complex and involved. The marketer must therefore be aware of the needs and wants of all the participants in the buying decision-making unit in a marketing strategy.

The actual purchase decision or the transaction of money for a product or service is only a part of this process. Much activity usually, but not always, precedes and follows the actual event of a purchase. Some purchases are very routine, some totally on impulse, some high value and infrequent, some low value. The process outlined in Figure 2.2 can be compressed, or stretched, and is always affected by a variety of factors.

Figure 2.2   The buying process

Need identification

↓

Search

↓

Evaluation

↓

Purchase

↓

Use

Need identification starts the process and buyers have many varied needs requiring satisfaction. These needs can be internally generated, such as hunger and thirst at the physical level, or status and self esteem at the psychological level. Alternatively they can be externally stimulated by a variety of factors, such as advertising or by salespeople. Needs are problems to be solved for buyers. Identifying what triggers or causes needs to develop, how they can be stimulated and ultimately satisfied is a key facet of business. The most common explanation of human needs and wants is contained in Maslow's hierarchy of needs (Figure 2.3), in which he sought to explain why people are driven by particular needs at particular times. He arranged needs in an order of priority, from the most important, to those of less importance. The theory is that an individual who has satisfied an important basic need will be motivated to move on to the next higher need in line, through a process of heightened expectation and perception. Thus a customer will adjust to the acquisition of products dependent on social, cultural and financial conditions.

Search processes begin when buyers attempt to satisfy their needs. They do this by collecting information, sometimes very superficially, sometimes passively, and on other occasions very actively and in great detail. The search depends on various factors including their own knowledge and experience, immediate or delayed gratification, risk, time, money and effort. Again, marketing activities can help to speed up or narrow down the search process by identifying the attributes perceived as most important by buyers and home in on these to solve the buyer's problem.

Evaluation by the buyer considers the alternatives, to select the best, that is, most suitable to satisfy their needs. This evaluation takes place at different levels between companies, products and brands and is neither permanent nor unequivocal. Salespeople can change or modify beliefs and attitudes buyers possess. They can provide information and persuasion which encourages buyers to select their product in preference to other competing alternatives.

Purchase normally follows evaluation although the buyer may change purchase intentions due to situational factors

Figure 2.3 Maslow's hierarchy of needs

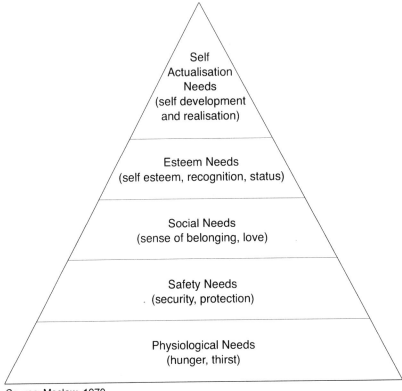

Source: Maslow, 1970

such as a special offer on alternative products or unforeseen changes since the evaluation was made. Also the purchase decisions may change if buying a trial quantity only or in price via credit. Different products, consumables of low value and consumer durables of higher value will vary in the extent of drift between purchase intention and decision. The level of expenditures and risk will influence the process at this stage.

Use is also important, in that if the need is satisfied adequately, re-purchase is likely and also positive word-of-mouth recommendations will be made to others. Similarly, dissatisfaction will have various negative effects with buyers and potential buyers in future purchase decisions.

THE PRODUCT

The product is the basic marketing element and includes all the features required to make an appeal to the customer market. The product is not only the physical or tangible elements but the whole bundle of benefits which the product or service represents. Consumers do not buy fragrant water, they buy perfume which has the capacity to make them feel and smell beautiful. Consumers do not buy drills, they buy the facility to make holes; and consumers do not buy T-shirts, they purchase fashion statements. Firms who are product or production-oriented often make this elementary mistake yet making the 'best' product, however that is defined, is seldom enough. You have to provide a satisfactory consumption experience and superior service. Firms who do not realise this end up making products – steam engines, vinyl records or linoleum – when customers prefer, or have been persuaded, to buy diesel engines, CDs or other forms of floor covering. Therefore the business and the product must reflect markets and customers in terms of benefits rather than in terms of product physical attributes. A paint manufacturer's business is really decorative materials, not paint; a brick manufacturer is in the building materials business; and an oil company is in the energy supply and distribution business. This is more than semantics and is vital for several reasons. First, changes in markets, nationally and internationally, are continuing to increase, making it essential to identify trends, adapt and react to change. Secondly, the essence of good business is to match what you do and what you produce to the needs of your customers. Thirdly, it is dangerous for the firm to enter new markets or produce new or additional products which are not part of a growth trend or in line with existing capabilities. Policies regarding the types of product should also be based on three subsidiary but core issues in marketing: the product life cycle, the Ansoff matrix and portfolio analysis.

The product life cycle bears token to the fact that products are vulnerable to change and have a finite life span. Public tastes change, technological advances take place and competition remains a constant threat. As Figure 2.4 shows,

Figure 2.4   The product life cycle concept

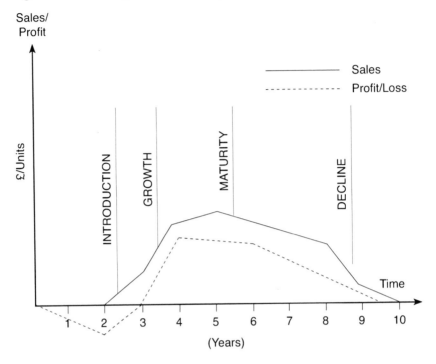

a product experiences slow sales at its launch; if successful, this leads into growth as it becomes known and appreciated. It reaches maturity when sales growth levels off and repeat purchases account for the majority of sales. Ultimately sales decline and new products and technologies enter the market. The product life cycle is based on the idea that products, like living organisms, are born, grow, mature and die. New products are introduced as substitutes for old products – for example, plastics replace wood or metal, calculators replace slide rules and steam engines replace horse power only to be replaced by diesel and electric power. The opportunity for new products may be because of rising costs for established products, changes in taste or fashion, shortages of raw materials or new innovation or technological change. The outcome of this process is that action must be considered for replacement products, to extend or improve existing products or to diversify into new areas of business.

In the case of a new product, when it is first introduced demand will grow only slowly. In some, indeed many, cases the resistance to change may result in failure and premature death. In other cases the natural rate of adoption is distorted by the policies or acceptance of distributors. New grocery products which are not accepted by the big four supermarkets mean instant failure, except as a small niche product. However, if customer needs have been correctly identified and matched by the product's benefits, the product will survive. This introductory stage usually makes a negative contribution to a firm's profits and in some cases, where development costs are high and the risk great, can mean not only temporary losses but a threat to the future viability of the firm.

In the growth stage, the product's advantages result in an increasing rate of acceptance by the market. Production expands, costs fall and, although competition may emerge, the product should prove profitable. At this stage it is expected that sales and profits are positive and growing. Expansion does not proceed unchecked and at some point demand will level out and the rate of profits increase begin to slow. This is the mature stage, which can sometimes be in two parts: first, when sales are still growing but at a much slower rate as competition is more intense; secondly, when sales begin to decline as the market reaches saturation. Inevitably, if unchecked sales and profits will decline.

This is a very simple and stylised version of a mythical product, which can also apply to a service or an idea such as a form of retailing. In some cases, with the benefit of hindsight, product life cycles can be drawn. The concept is not without its critics and there is a degree of controversy among experts over the use of a product life cycle analysis, because of the uncertainty of tracking its passage through the cycle and measuring its impact. Further, products are not biological and this process can and will be affected by managerial decisions about the product and how it is marketed. The main difficulty is in defining a product. A product may refer to a product category such as alcoholic drinks or tobacco, to a product form within a category such as whisky or filter cigarettes, to a brand such as Famous Grouse or Silk Cut. The life cycle for each is quite different. The concept should therefore be treated with caution and used as a general indication of product performance. Support for the concept comes from theories of innovation and diffusion which do follow an S-shaped cover as products are adopted by consumers.

The Ansoff matrix is really a strategic tool but it has great significance for product decisions. The risks and costs associated with new products and new markets are high and a firm must assess the options it has very carefully. Ansoff (1957) identified four basic strategies: market penetration, product development, market development and diversification (see Figure 2.5).

Figure 2.5   The Ansoff matrix

	Current products	**New products**
Current markets	Market penetration strategy	Product development strategy
New markets	Market development strategy	Diversification strategy

Source: Ansoff, 1987

Market penetration involves increasing business with existing customers for existing products. This is an attempt to increase market share at the expense of competitors usually by means of short-run tactics of price cutting or additional promotional expenditure. In some cases it can be achieved by policies of product improvement, more effective target marketing, called niche marketing, or in business-to-business marketing by networking.

Product development involves adding new items or new products to an existing range in the same market type or area. It is often difficult to predict how acceptable new products will be in the market and the likely effect on existing products. Will the market expand or remain static, merely shifting from the old to the new with little effect on overall sales and profits?

Market development or extension involves expansion through existing products in new areas, very often new countries and sometimes new or different market segments.

Diversification involves both market and product development. This approach involves the greatest risk since there is a lack of knowledge on two fronts and evidence suggests this is more often a route to failure than success. Many companies embark on over-ambitious schemes and are forced to pull out. Diversification requires careful market appraisal and, in particular, careful competitor reaction assessment. Strong motivation and significant resources may be required.

Portfolio analysis provides the information base for the development and evaluation of marketing plans and product policy decisions in particular. Its principal role is resource allocation in the management of a product, but it also provides an input to the decision on the current and future mix and balance of a business portfolio. The best-known approach to portfolio analysis is the Boston Consulting Group growth share matrix, known more familiarly as the 'Boston box'. The matrix is used to plot the position of business units or products, according to their individual market growth and market share, relative to the largest competitor.

The layout is shown in Figure 2.6. The matrix is divided into four parts, each indicating a different sector of business. The horizontal scale is logarithmic and the dividing mark between 'HIGH' and 'LOW' is 1. Thus a relative market share of 0.1 indicates a 10% sales volume. The vertical scale is in percentages, with the mean between 'HIGH' and 'LOW' being 10%. In addition, the portfolio should balance the cash-generating and cash-demanding products. The four business sector types are categorised as follows.

Figure 2.6 The Boston box (growth share matrix)

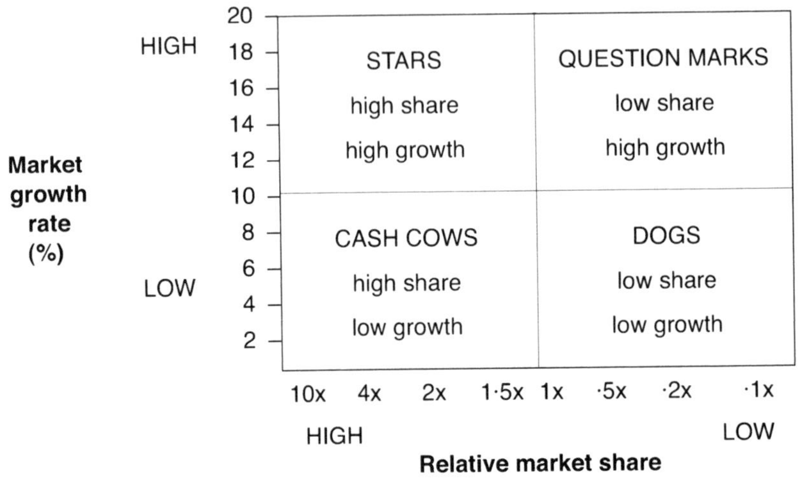

Source: Boston Consulting Group, 1977

- *Question marks* Businesses which operate in a high growth market with a low relative market share. It requires a large cash flow to invest in plant, equipment and personnel to keep up with and overtake market developments. The question is whether to keep on investing or to withdraw from the market.
- *Stars* Businesses which are market leaders in a high growth market. Stars generate but also consume large amounts of cash and, provided market share is maintained, stars become cash cows.
- *Cash cows* Businesses which retain a high share of the market in a static or falling rate of market growth, generate large amounts of cash, with relatively little outlay.
- *Dogs* Businesses which have a weak market share in a low growth market. They generate either a low profit or a loss. A decision is necessary whether to hold on or phase out of the market.

Once you have established your matrix, the next task is to determine what to do. There are four possible options:

- *Build* Increase market share to strengthen your position. (A long-term objective suitable for question marks aiming to be stars.)

- *Hold* Maintain market share. (Appropriate for strong cash cows to yield a large cash flow.)

- *Harvest* Increase short-term cash flow. (This is appropriate for weak cash cows, question marks and dogs.)

- *Divest* Get rid of profit drain. (Appropriate for dogs and question marks that are becoming a liability.)

SEGMENTATION

Your business has to have a focus for marketing to be effective and successful. An important feature of your marketing plan will concern the market segments your marketing intends to target. Segmentation divides the large, varied, potential buying market into smaller groupings, each with broadly similar patterns of needs and characteristics. Breaking the market into these more manageable parts also makes your task much more precise and therefore much more cost-effective for your marketing and promotional plan.

It is very seldom, if at all nowadays, that a product or marketing approach will appeal to the general needs and wants of the broad spectrum of the buying public. This is why, of the three marketing approaches – mass marketing, product-variety marketing and target marketing – it is the target marketing method which is most favoured. The potential benefits of a well-constructed segmentation strategy can be considerable. A business should be able to establish and strengthen its position in the market, build knowledge of its market sector, develop customer loyalty and make it more difficult for competitors to challenge.

Segmentation defines the purchasers or users of your product, who become your primary target. There may also be secondary targets, who are influenced by the primary focus. For example, if you were marketing a product to the educational sector, it would not only influence the teachers, but also administrators and, in particular, budget holders.

The role of influence should not be overlooked in your targeting and is best illustrated by the involvement of a wife in the selection of clothes by her husband. In this case the husband is the purchaser and user, but the wife cannot be ignored and therefore becomes a secondary target. If your user is not the purchaser, which becomes the primary target? Do you target both? Remember it is very difficult to market two primary markets effectively. In consideration of the problem, you should take note of the following factors:

- measurability – or the degree to which market size, market potential and market characteristics can be accurately estimated and determined;
- accessibility – or the ease with which it will be possible to reach customers in a given segment;
- substantiality – so that identified segments can produce sufficient volume and profit.

Segmentation is based on a wide variety of factors, the majority of which can be grouped into four main categories. These variables can be broken down by survey and analysis into a clear identification of the major segments in the market.

- geographic – country, region or even cities, perhaps also by climate or population;
- demographic – age, sex, education, occupation, income, religion, family size, nationality;
- behavioural – attitudes, knowledge, benefits, buyer readiness, user status (such as heavy and light users or brand loyal versus brand switchers);
- psychographic – social class, lifestyle or personality.

Particular segments can also be used in industrial or business to business markets. Again geographic segments, large versus small users or group buying factors are the most likely to be used.

The market segmentation stage uses consumer research to segment the market in accordance with the variables shown earlier and the consumer attitude to the product(s) being marketed. This information is then used to fashion similarly-oriented segments of consumers by analysis. The final part is profiling the segments on a dominant distinguishing characteristic of the group. The stages are shown in Table 2.1.

Table 2.1   The segmentation process

Segment the market	Target the market	Position the product
Identify the segmentation variable factors	Evaluate the attraction of each segment	Identify position concepts for each target segment
Segment the market by analysis	Select the target segments	Select, develop and signal the chosen position concept

The targeting process must evaluate the segment size and growth prospects, relative to the way you want to conduct your business. Size is not only physical; it also relates to sales volume. The attraction a segment holds for you is the profit perspective and market possibilities, but you also have to judge and take into consideration the following threats in Table 2.2.

Your selection of the target segment(s) offers a number of options:

- *Single-segment concentration* is vulnerable to competitor challenge and customer uncertainty, but does allow concentration of effort for a business with limited funds.

- *Selective segmentation,* in a number of attractive segments, permits a business to diversify the risk.

- *Product specialisation* to a number of segments places the emphasis on the reputation of the product.

Table 2.2   Segmentation threats and actions

Threat	Remarks
Segment rivalry	Too many competitors in the segment
New competitor entry	The segment attracts new competitors as well as you and affects the effort and resources you have to expend for market-share
Threat of substitute products	Which may overshadow your product and price
Threats from buyers and suppliers	Strong buying power tends to force prices down, demand more quality and service and encourage competition. Suppliers of material may raise prices and reduce quality and are in a strong position if they are organised and there is no alternative to them

- *Market specialisation* serves many needs of a particular segment and carries an array of products.
- *Full market coverage*, serving all customer segments, is reserved for only the very large businesses.

The positioning of the product will place your business image and product value at a level you wish to target your segment(s), in comparison to that of your competitors. For instance, you may wish to emphasise your 'high technology position', or a 'high quality position'. Whatever the position you choose, it must establish some sort of advantage over your competitors. It should also be noted that, by positioning your product, you will be targeting a niche within your target segment which is particularly concerned with the product position, e.g. those interested in high quality.

The final part of positioning is telling the market your business's positioning concept. Basically this means building and advertising your competitive advantage over competitors. A comparative analysis will define a number of attributes for evaluation.

Table 2.3   The competitive advantage selection

1	2	3	4	5	6	7
Competitive advantage	Business position	Competitor position	Importance to customer in improving position	Affordability and speed	Competitor ability to to improve position	Recommended action
–	(1–10)	(1–10)	(H–M–L)	(H–M–L)	(H–M–L)	–
Technology	8	8	L	L	M	Hold
Cost	6	8	H	M	M	Monitor
Quality	8	6	L	L	H	Monitor
Service	4	3	H	H	L	Invest

1 (Low) – 10 (High)   H – High   M – Medium   L – Low

Source: Adapted from Kotler, 2003

Table 2.3 gives an example of four of the more common sources of advantage, comparing technology, cost, quality and service, and it is the judgement on the interrelationship between the scores allotted to each which determines the recommended action. Each has an equal position on technology and the question is, whether the business can gain by improving, compared against the cost of doing so. The low and medium measurements of the other factors add weight to the decision to 'hold'. The competitor has a better position on cost (8–6), whereas the business offers higher quality (8–6). What should the business do? What do the customers want? Are improvements affordable? What are the competitors going to do? These questions indicate the deductive process which must be applied to the model, to enable your business to seek the best competitive advantage.

A suitable position in a target market is assessed by whether a profit can be made in the market segment, whether potential sales in the segment will increase, decline or remain constant, what the competition is and is likely to do and where the basis of any comparative advantage lies for your firm.

THE MARKETING MIX

The marketing mix is the term given to the elements of marketing activity and was popularised as a combination of the four principal planning factors in the marketing process, namely the 4 Ps – Product, Price, Place and Promotion. There are a number of other permutations possible and some marketing experts add a fifth P, that of People, while those in service businesses suggest process and physical evidence need to be added in what is termed 'the seven Ps of services marketing'.

- **Product** – includes all aspects of the product: production, management, development, brand image and packaging.

- **Price** – embraces the cost of the product to the customer: pricing structure, discounts, financial incentives.

- **Place** – the physical location, distribution, customer service, area of operations.

- **Promotion** – the selling, advertising, sales promotion, merchandising, public relations.

- **People** – covers the attitudes, aspirations, influences, beliefs, values, institutional or product loyalty.

There are a number of external factors which affect the marketing mix, such as political, legal, economic and environmental issues. The marketing planning process has little or no direct influence over these, but must take account of their impact. A further aspect is the evolution of cultural and social development as it applies to a product. All these various factors combine to make the marketing situation so variable that it has to be continuously monitored and adjusted, to ensure that supply meets demand and makes a healthy balance sheet. We will return to these factors as part of our planning process.

CRITICAL SUCCESS FACTORS

Critical success factors are those current sources of advantage which give you a competitive edge and hence a superior performance over your opposition. Financial criteria used to dominate the choice of success factors; however, quality, service and value now have equal if not superior emphasis. The choice of factors is a direct consequence of the application of Pareto's Law, or the 80/20 rule. It is often asserted that 80% of inventory movements within a business result from 20% of the items stocked, 80% of sales volume comes from 20% of customers and 80% of profits are derived from 20% of product lines. Therefore by controlling an inventory focused on 20% of stock items, controlling the level of sales by looking after 20% of key customers and making cost savings from eliminating unnecessary control of the 80% of items making up 20% of stock issues, can have a significant impact on organisational effectiveness.

Critical success factors have a number of characteristics: they can change quickly, they are difficult to predict, they require a prompt response to any market change, and their effects can be measured. A list of typical factors include: profitability; market position; productivity; product leadership; personnel development; employee attitude; public responsibilities; balance between long-term and short-term goals.

Your assessment of critical success factors should not relate to individual elements of marketing, but be aggregated where possible to take account of overlapping interests. Advertising can hardly be separated from the other elements of the marketing mix and will influence the selling task, the nature of the product and the price. Therefore the appropriate point to consider its effectiveness is at the level of the marketing programme, which integrates these interests.

You should therefore develop distinct competencies, appropriate to your business, which will implement your overall marketing strategy. They must be tailored to the specific characteristics of your situation and be in concert with your strategic business plans, e.g. a focus on short-term maximum profit may damage long-term strategy/objectives.

MARKETING INFORMATION SYSTEM

Figure 2.7 Marketing information system

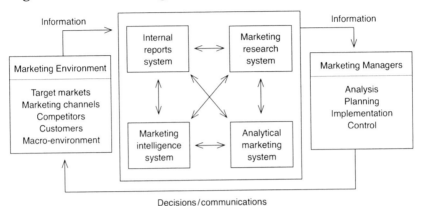

Source: Adapted from Kotler (1997)

The collection, processing and dissemination of data is one of the most important factors in marketing. A marketing information system embraces internal reports, intelligence requirements, research and analysis and is central to establishing competitive advantage and market success. The integral elements are mutually supporting and interlocking, as shown in Figure 2.7. It provides an excellent means of integrating information from a variety of sources and providing a current, continuously updated database for your business.

The internal reports system underlines the need for timeliness and accuracy in handling the procedural aspects of business organisation. Reports on orders, sales, stock levels and invoices keep managerial staff informed and up to date on the results and progress of business. Points to note are the relevance of the information and its volume. The system will require periodic review to ensure that the information meets requirements and is kept at a manageable level of volume.

Marketing intelligence gains information on the developments within the marketing environment. The information comes from journals, trade publications, newspapers, conversation with those involved in the particular market (i.e. customers, distributors and suppliers) and those in the business. Increasingly, many of these sources are now internet-based. However, sales personnel are a particular grouping which has the potential to gain a great deal of business intelligence. The influence of routine reports on market intelligence should ensure a flow of information from these outlets to the managerial level and a subsequent dissemination of the information collected, circulated to all staff levels of the business, will encourage continued participation.

Market research originates from primary and secondary data. Secondary data is readily available from existing sources such as business publications, commercial information, official statistics and on-line sources. Its advantages are that it is quickly available and less costly to obtain; however, the information may be outdated, inaccurate and incomplete. Primary data is more costly to obtain, but will be current and can be gathered and prepared in a format to suit your purpose. It will come from customer interviews/surveys, observation, focus group research and experimentation. The most common data collection device is the questionnaire, which can be constructed to suit the research. This flexibility comes at a price, because care and attention have to be given to the construction of the questions. They must be clearly expressed, free from ambiguity and pre-tested to ensure accuracy.

The analytical marketing system is a logical progression from the data readily available, within a business. Statistical models can be framed to suit requirements and enhance the marketing manager's ability to make decisions.

It is important that you use the information connected with your business in an efficient and structured manner. Gathering information for information's sake will be counter-productive and time-consuming and will not assist you in the goals you have set yourself. A marketing information system, designed along the lines of the system described in this section, should prove an asset in your marketing development.

3 MARKETING ANALYSIS

I had six faithful serving men, they taught me all I knew, their names were,

Where and What and When and How and Why and Who

Rudyard Kipling

No matter what the nature of a business, it will not flourish, or even survive, if it operates in a vacuum of knowledge concerning its business interests. Information is the oxygen of the marketing process. The collection and analysis of information lies at the root of successful marketing in support of future action and future plans. It consists of four elements: marketing analysis; customer analysis; competitor analysis; and an analysis of strengths and weaknesses of the business in the context of external threats and opportunities (SWOT analysis). It takes stock of the situation and examines the marketing factors which lie at the heart of business development, as demonstrated in Figure 3.1.

Figure 3.1   The collection and analysis of information

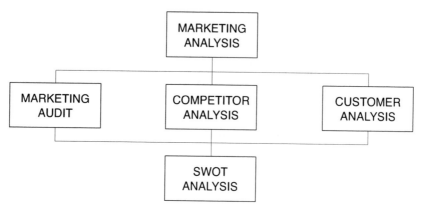

MARKETING AUDIT

The marketing audit looks at all the major activities of a business in a comprehensive and systematic fashion. It should be held periodically and, to get the best, unbiased results, should be conducted in an objective and independent manner. The outcome should be discussed at a senior level with those who have authority within the business. The audit is an assessment of your business within its working environment and, as a process, consists of a number of steps.

The first step is to establish the operating network within which the business conducts its affairs by placing it as the centre of focus and connecting it to every party with which it has an exchange relationship. The nature of exchange, which may be positive, negative or mutually satisfying, is immaterial at this stage; the important factor is to understand the interchange between the parties. A further consideration is that there are different exchange mechanisms, which are not necessarily connected to pure commerce – the so-called stakeholder concept. After taking due account of all the different factors, you should now construct your particular network of stakeholders and relationships. An illustrative example of a typical network, concerning a hospital, is shown in Figure 3.2.

The next step in the audit is to examine the factors of influence currently impacting on your business. These are divided into internal and external influences, governing finance, personnel and production, within six spheres of interest: environment, strategy, organisation, systems, productivity and function. These components and the key issues affecting them will now be examined. The questions: 'Does it affect me?', 'In what way?', 'What shall I do about it?', 'So what?', are indicative of the interrogative process you must go through in each sphere of interest, to gain a qualitative overall judgement of your current position and future development. To answer these questions, let us consider each sphere of interest in turn.

Environment looks at macro influences (those more general and distant to the business, over which it has little

Figure 3.2 An illustrative network – hospital

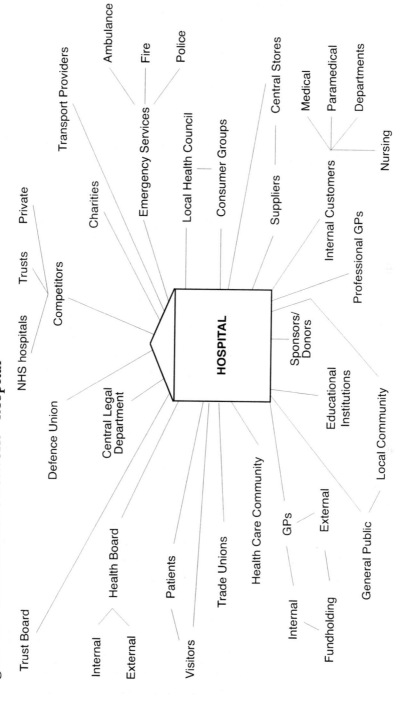

control) and micro influences (those nearest to and most intimately involved in the business). The principal **macro-environmental** issues and the sort of issues raised and questions you should address are as follows:

- *Demography*   You should be aware of the size of your target population and any changes taking place. It is inevitable that you will be dealing with a wide range of ethnicity and consequently consumer tastes. It will be particularly important to stay in tune with consumer developments and trends. It never fails to amaze how basic trends such as ageing population, declining birth rates, all very predictable, are often ignored yet impact on a great many businesses – see Figure 3.3.

- *Economy*   Economic conditions have a direct effect on the marketing process and you will have an obvious interest in growth rates in the countries in which you operate and other economic conditions such as inflation and prices, the effect of the economy on savings and income and, of course, foreign exchange rates.

- *Ecology*   The emphasis on conservation of natural resources and energy and pollution matters is unlikely to diminish in the foreseeable future and sub-issues on these topics will have to be monitored closely from your business perspective.

- *Technology*   Technological changes and developments are continually happening and have to be monitored very carefully because of the speed with which they occur. The introduction of product substitutes is a particular threat. The impact of electronic commerce and the internet has had a huge impact albeit more dramatic in some industries than others.

- *Politics*   Political legislation has a considerable impact on employment, safety and product policies. You will have to know and keep your knowledge up to date on the key legislative issues affecting your business.

Figure 3.3   Europe's changing population (forecast growth rates to 2020)

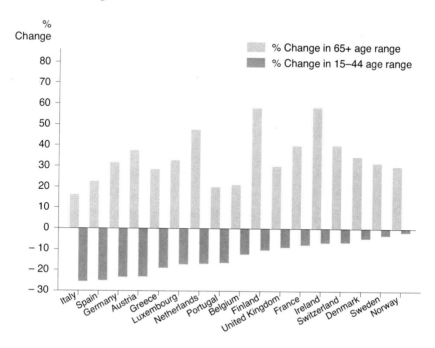

Source: National statistical offices. *European Marketing Pocket Book*, 2000 (Henley-on-Thames, UK: NTC Publications, 2000), p. 10. NTC Publications Ltd.

- *Legal issues*   The legal aspects of employment conditions and issues such as product liability must be clearly understood and enforced to the best of your ability.

- *Social/cultural issues*   It is always a considerable advantage to be familiar with the attitudes, values and lifestyles existing within your customer base. These are constantly changing and evolving and can significantly impact on your business.

The **micro-environmental** factors include the following:

- *Markets*   What is their size? Where are they based geographically? Is there market growth? Are they profitable? Do you have market priorities? Have you developed market segments? Have you targeted these segments?

- *Customers* Do you know who they are? Do you know what they want? Do you know why they buy? Have you done a customer analysis?

- *Competitors* Do you have any information on them? Do you know their objectives, strengths, weaknesses? Do you know their market share? Have you done a competitor analysis?

- *Distributors/dealers* Are they cost-effective? Are they efficient? Are distribution channels effective and sufficient?

- *Suppliers* Have you investigated new or alternative sources? Are resources sufficient? Are changes necessary?

- *Advertising/PR* Is it effective? Is it creative? Are there sufficient opportunities? Does it follow trends?

Strategy is the second factor and addresses what you intend to do and how you intend to accomplish it. There are three broad areas of interest:

- *Mission* Your business mission must be clear, feasible and consistent with your overall plans and strategy. It will be addressed later in the book in much more detail, but essentially you must be clearly committed to a course of positive action.

- *Objectives/goals* These will establish measurable milestones you wish to achieve in the future. They will have to be in balance with your mission and the way you propose to run your business. They have to be believable, to encourage and motivate your staff and be attainable.

- *Strategy* The third factor points the way forward. It envelops all your planning and the execution of your plans. It looks at checks and controls on progress, market segmentation and is the strand of continuity, binding the components of marketing together.

Organisation This is probably the principal key factor in your overall audit. A sound organisational framework within your business is a cornerstone of success. A structured management system and well-trained staff, with authority delegated to appropriate levels, will motivate personnel and encourage team effort. There must be good communication among all staff and the establishment of training standards and programmes will ensure a high skill level. Staff promotional incentives should also be considered for career development and staff suggestion schemes for business improvement should be encouraged. The institution of job descriptions for each member of staff is an effective method of letting staff know what is expected of them and allows you to measure their performance against a standard. It is also important to let your staff know how they are performing their tasks in relation to the standards you have set. A staff audit, which will formally examine these features and collate them in a single report, is an essential part of the overall audit and a useful management tool for day-to-day use.

Systems Many of the checks and controls in your business can be made much more efficient and reliable by the use of the management information system. The need for information is a recurring theme in marketing and investment in information systems will greatly assist the collection and analysis of marketing information. Information must be accurate and timely and presented in an efficient and understandable way. It should be distributed as widely as you think necessary within the confines of your business, on the basis that if someone needs to know, then they should be informed. The way information is gathered, disseminated and used is a characteristic of the market-oriented organisation.

The flexibility of information systems allows you to forecast, measure, monitor, validate and analyse product performance and potential; also to research, test and develop new products and check on the quality control issues concerning the product, service, information mix which is now such an important part of modern marketing.

Productivity A review of productivity will examine your markets and determine the action you should take to gain the maximum benefit. It will cover expansion of markets, withdrawal from unprofitable channels, or contraction of business in times of economic hardship. The focus is firmly on product profitability and cost-effectiveness of channels of distribution and of the chosen market segments. Part of this may well be a coherent product elimination system.

Function The function review will look at what you are doing in your current business operations regarding your products, prices, distribution, sales force and advertising and promotion. The types of question which will be addressed are:

- Am I meeting my objectives?
- Do I need to adjust products, prices?
- Is my distribution giving good service and cost-effective?
- Is the sales force operating well, achieving targets?
- Am I getting value for money in advertising and promotion?
- Am I reaching the target audience?

The marketing analysis of your current business performance is an extremely important measure, because most future marketing actions are dictated by its findings. It has to be conducted in a systematic and comprehensive fashion, without any bias or preconception. It will also cost time and money to carry out and must therefore be treated seriously, if you are to receive the maximum benefit from it. It is also important to record all the information gathered as a reference point for research and defining future marketing action.

COMPETITOR ANALYSIS

This is a measurement of your strengths and weaknesses against those of your business rivals and what it is that attracts customers to you and not them, and vice versa. Competitors will have a significant impact on the conduct of your business, therefore you must not fail to take account of their position in the market, vis-à-vis your own. Competition comes from all businesses operating in the same product category, delivering the same service, or competing for the same spending source.

There is a delicate balance to be drawn between you and your competitors, which is a matter of judgement rather than decree. It is a question of how much effort and energy you wish to direct against them compared to promoting your own business and what you wish to achieve at the end. The existence of competitors is sometimes an advantage in sharing markets, e.g. a badly run competitor business will comparatively enhance the prospects of your well-run business. Likewise, a competitor you drive out of business may be taken over by another and create a bigger opposition for you to compete against. Only by examination and analysis will you be able to make the judgement.

A competitor analysis will prevent you being taken by surprise or being overtaken in the market. It will also give you a lead on competitor capabilities, objectives and failings. Information is again the key to addressing the issue and you must ask the following questions:

- Who are you competing against?
- What are their objectives?
- What strategies do they employ, and how successful are they?
- What are their strengths and weaknesses?
- How do they react to competition?

The answers should provide an indication of what you are up against and start you thinking what to do about it. The development of an information data base on your competitors is a sensible course of action. At the outset, you must identify your competitors and set up the data system. Data has then to be collected from a cross-section of departments in your business, e.g. sales, marketing, engineering, etc. Data falls into three broad categories: recorded, observed, and opportunity.

- Recorded data is readily available from a variety of sources. Government statistics, business and trade press and technical journals, various official reports and public documents are typical of where recorded data may be found.

- Observed data collection is concerned with what your competitors are doing to advance their business interests, in terms of price, promotion, manufacturing and service. It can go as far as a detailed component examination of the competitors' products.

- Opportunity data may be obtained by word-of-mouth, overheard, or by surreptitious testing of competitors' sales practice and product. Exhibitions, distributors, suppliers and even disaffected employees all have information which may help.

Once the information has been obtained, it must be analysed, assessed and distributed to an appropriate level in your business for consideration of further action. There are various areas of interest in which it is advantageous to gain information on your competitors. Some of these are shown in Table 3.1 with examples of specific interest items in each, which can be enlarged upon to suit the requirements of your particular business.

Table 3.1   Competitor information

Sales	Advertising/promotion	Finance
Product lines, trends, market share	Expenditure, effectiveness, literature, sales promotion	Margins, resources, position
Customer	**Distribution and channels**	**Management**
Loyalty, satisfaction, repeat business, image/ profile	Networks, costs, flexibility, sales force size and capability, after sales service, stock policy, depots/sales offices	Objectives, strategies, attitudes, plans, skills
Product		**General**
Range, performance, new products, research and development		Employee relations, buildings, equipment, market commitment
	Price	
	Structure, discounts	

The information gathered from your competitor analysis gives you a better sense of what you are up against and what you should do about it. Understanding your opposition goes a long way to defining appropriate action and the likely reaction; and the information system you devise must not only provide the necessary knowledge, but also stay within the legal and ethical bounds of obtaining such information. Your approach to competitors should always be pragmatic and constructive and avoid emotional extremes, which are likely to cloud your judgement. It is always better to be a tough, fair competitor and seek accommodation in a market, rather than the distraction of confrontation and divisive market warfare.

CUSTOMER ANALYSIS

The key to customer retention and customer loyalty is customer satisfaction and this can only be brought about by a thorough understanding and knowledge of who your customers are and what they want from your business. It has already been stated that a business has to define customer needs from the customer point of view. Meeting those needs is the challenge facing you. The attraction of new customers and the retention of current customers are major factors in marketing. New customers are expensive to attract and it becomes a major preoccupation to retain their custom as well as that of current customers.

It is also most important that the dissatisfaction of customers is uncovered in the process. A substantial proportion of customer dissatisfaction is not generally made known to a business directly, but creates a significant impact on public opinion from word-of-mouth transmission of complaints to relatives and friends. The encouragement and sympathetic treatment of customer complaints can greatly enhance the standing of your business with the general public.

There are two principal customer groupings. One is the customer who buys on an individual basis. The second is the organisational or business buyer. The main difference between the two is that business buyers do not buy for personal consumption, they buy to make money, reduce costs or fulfil an obligation, e.g. to conform to pollution control requirements. They are fewer in number compared to the consumer market, however they buy more and develop much closer links with their sources of supply. This customer loyalty has to be matched by your business dependability, product reliability and pricing competitiveness.

There are three main categories of business purchase. One is a straightforward reorder as a matter of routine, based on past buying satisfaction. The second is a modified reorder, in which the business modifies aspects of the purchase, delivery dates or product specifications. The third category is a major challenge and opportunity facing the marketer, that of a new purchase order. The purchaser will be buying for the first time and special attention will be required to achieve success. Progress will develop through a number of stages over an extended time frame and cover such items as the product order, quantities, price limits, delivery service and so on.

The focus on product considerations must not overlook the impact of human factors. Interpersonal and individual relationships are equally important in establishing a rapport between the marketer and the business purchaser and will be a considerable advantage over your competitors. Lastly, you must obtain a thorough knowledge of the organisation doing the buying, its objectives, policies, structures and systems.

The buying behaviour of the individual customer is as varied as the range of products available for purchase. The primary object in the process is to understand how customers make their buying decision. It is influenced by cultural, social, personal and psychological factors which, although largely uncontrollable by marketing, have to be taken into account. During the chain of events leading to a purchase, a decision-making process unfolds. Table 3.2 shows the outline of the various decisions and considerations the customer has to take during the process, which should enable you to bring as much of a marketing influence to bear as possible.

The influence you can bring to bear during the process of the customer's acquisition of information can be significant

Table 3.2 Purchase decision process

Stage	Customer reaction
Problem recognition	Stimulation of needs – What needs? What brought them about? How did they lead to a product?
Information search	Receptive to information about product. Information sources: personal, commercial, public, experience. Reads promotional material, speaks to friends.
Evaluation of alternatives	Comparative assessment on: product attribute, brand expectation, utility, preference, judgement.
Purchase decision	Form a preference. Influence of others. Affordable. Perceived risk. Executive decision: brand, vendor, quantity, timing, payment method.
Post-purchase behaviour	Buyer satisfaction: performance, expectations, service.

and you should be aware of the different types of buying behaviour that a customer is likely to exhibit and gauge your reaction accordingly. A key question is whether the purchase is a low or high-involvement purchase. In fact four types of buying behaviour, based on the degree of buyer involvement and the difference between brands, have been identified:

Complex buying behaviour occurs when a customer is highly involved in a purchase, which is expensive, infrequent, risky and self-expressive. The marketer has to understand how the customer gains information on the product and subsequently applies it on an evaluation of the product. The marketer must also appreciate the customer's desire to enlist support in influencing the purchase decision.

Disparity-reducing buying behaviour is where the customer is again highly involved in a purchase of similar parameters to the complex buying example, but sees little difference between brands. After the purchase the customer experiences disquiet that the purchase was not as good as previously thought and that other products were more favourable (in academic jargon this is termed post-cognitive dissonance). The customer then seeks to justify the purchase decision to reduce the dissonance or disquiet. The role for the marketer in such a case is to help the purchaser feel good about the purchase.

Habitual buying behaviour is characterised by low customer involvement and an absence of significant brand difference. Customers do not form an attitude towards a brand but select it on the basis of familiarity, not conviction of its worth. Marketers of low-involvement products can use price and sales promotion and low-key advertising to assist the product, but expectations of raised consumer involvement will remain low. Market leaders will encourage habitual buying behaviour and sponsor reminder advertising.

Variety-seeking buying behaviour has low customer involvement but significant brand differences. It is typified by brand-switching for variety rather than dissatisfaction. Variety-seeking can be encouraged by lower prices, deals, coupons, and feature advertising.

Input to your customer analysis will be obtained from the marketing audit and help to put together a composite picture of your customer base. Periodic customer surveys and the maintenance of customer records will further contribute to your overall knowledge; however, it is the measures for customer satisfaction, applied to the knowledge of your customers, which will result in the most benefits for your business.

STRENGTHS, WEAKNESSES, OPPORTUNITIES AND THREATS (SWOT) ANALYSIS

The SWOT analysis is the final element of the marketing analysis and is an internal and external examination of your business. Strengths and weaknesses are the internal factors and opportunities and threats represent the external factors.

The aim is to increase strengths, reduce weakness, eliminate threats and exploit opportunities. The SWOT provides core information by identifying the positive and negative aspects of a business, focusing on the importance of human attitudes and capabilities as well as specific marketing factors. It will incorporate much of the data you have gathered in the preceding analyses and help to qualify and confirm such findings. You should conduct the SWOT analysis on a periodic basis, because information of this nature does not remain constant and the components are important enough to keep up to date. As far as possible it should be research based and it is important that it is not subjective and opinionated.

Each factor raised in connection with the analysis will not have an equal bearing or value. It will therefore have to be rated in accordance with a scale of major to minor importance. In the case of your strengths and weaknesses, Figure 3.4 shows a suggested layout and allocates to each item raised an importance level ranging from a low of '1' to a high of '5'.

In a similar fashion, Figure 3.5 shows a suggested layout for opportunities and threats and measures, each through low to medium to high.

The results of your analysis will provide a very important assessment of your business and lay the foundations for your various marketing plans in your progressive planning. Some examples of the more common topics raised in a SWOT analysis are listed below, to provide an illustration of the contents.

- **Strengths** Dynamic management; excellent reputation; quality product/service; trained, motivated staff; customer loyalty; flexible working practices; advertising/presentational skills; state-of-the-art equipment.

- **Weaknesses** Situations of weakness create problems for a business and are essentially negative. They should be expressed in a short, concise format. Typical problem areas are: lack of training for staff/

Figure 3.4   Analysis of strengths and weaknesses

Number	Strengths	Importance level 1 (low) – 5 (high)

Number	Weaknesses	Importance level 1 (low) – 5 (high)

Notes: (1) number each entry; (2) keep each comment brief; (3) assign an importance level in the range 1 (low) – 5 (high).

Figure 3.5   Assessment of opportunities and threats

Number	Strengths	Importance level 1 (low) – 5 (high)

Number	Weaknesses	Importance level 1 (low) – 5 (high)

management; lack of resources; inefficiency of staff; high overheads; falling sales; lack of forward planning; ineffective advertising; lack of customer service; reliance on government grants.

- **Opportunities** They are developed from strengths or positive circumstances. A combination of circumstances may create an opportunity. As an example, an aggressive marketing programme, advertised through mass media to a target audience, is the sort of coalition of effort which will lead to an opportunity. Opportunities will capitalise on your strengths and in addition will identify areas in which to exploit the weakness of your competitors. Typical opportunities are: new technology; expansion of trade in product; small number of competitors; investment in training; improved promotion prospects; wide range of product/prices; gaining repeat business; achieving quality standards; overseas development.

- **Threats** Economic recession; many competitors; falling volume market/sales; no development plan; market sensitivities; trade embargoes; legislation; ease of competitor entry into market.

The SWOT analysis provides the means of assessing the practical aspects of your business in a logical and structured way. The assessment has to be pragmatic and balance all the relevant facts. Items listed must have a bearing on your business and be of sufficient importance to warrant some form of action on them, although you may be able to strike a comparative balance between the positive and negative aspects because not every deficiency or weakness may be critical enough to be neutralised or corrected.

It is therefore very important to examine the totality of the points you list in the SWOT analysis and deduce the overall impact within each segment. Very often it is the cumulative, not the individual, effect of factors which is significant. This deduction will help to point you in the direction best suited for your business and bring your analysis to a logical conclusion.

The marketing analysis should conclude with sufficient information and assessment to form the basis for a sound planning process. It must provide enough factual knowledge to justify your future aims and ambitions and at the same time provide the evidence for corrective action of your business shortcomings, all of which can be incorporated into the marketing planning process.

4 THE MARKETING PLANNING PROCESS

Plans are nothing, planning is everything

Dwight Eisenhower

Following the judgement from the marketing analysis, you should now be in a position to start the planning process. The starting point is an expression of the corporate values of the business, integrating business objectives and bonding the various diverse elements such as human resources, geographic location, programmes and strategies into a single concentrated statement of your mission. Although many are cynical of vision/mission statements for a business, perhaps regarding it as 'motherhood and apple pie', it is important that business leaders address basic questions concerning their business:

- What business are we actually in ?
- What should our business be in the future?

These two questions provide the corporate mission which guides the activities of our business. While the questions are simple the answers are sometimes extremely difficult to define accurately. This is a process whereby markets are matched to resources and vice versa; and ultimately the strategic intent is translated into goals and objectives. Six subsidiary yet equally key questions need to be asked and answered at this stage:

- What might we do given our business environment?
- What can we do given our ability and competence?
- What do we as managers really want to do?

- What should we do given social, ethical and political constraints?
- Who is our customer?
- How do we create value for our customer?

Remember, firms who adopt a product-oriented or inward-looking stance in relation to their business, or firms who do not address these questions, can expect that product sales will eventually decline and markets will shrink as the external and competitive environment changes. Further, they will be operating without any real purpose.

VALUES AND MISSION STATEMENT FOR THE BUSINESS

It is important to have a statement of values or 'a mission' as a means of concentrating on the definitive issues on which to base business aims, objectives and strategies from the present to the future. It is a statement which not only encompasses the future pattern of a business, but also the needs of customers and guidance and direction for all staff levels in the business. It must provide a sense of purpose, set standards and provide motivation for the staff. The characteristics of a values/mission statement are brevity, precision and realism, focusing on specific and achievable targets. It must take a long-term, enduring perspective of the business in the domain in which it operates and highlight the distinctive and important values it wishes the staff of the business to aspire to.

The statement will have to take account of the views of three main groups involved with the business:

- Internal stakeholders: owners, managers, shareholders, unions and employees.
- External stakeholders: financial community, trade associations, government.
- Market-place stakeholders: customers, competitors, creditors, suppliers.

The constructive involvement of all three groups should result in a balanced, composite statement. Naturally, the evolving nature of business will force change on the statement. New products, new markets, changing conditions, will require a response over time to maintain an accurate reflection of business goals. The value proposition must therefore remain a living document.

As an example of the topics to be covered and an expression of aims and desires, a typical values/mission statement for an engineering firm could read:

- to provide the best quality, price and range of choice to our customers
- to maintain excellence and leadership in the development and manufacture of goods
- to achieve the highest standards of friendly, efficient customer service
- to offer staff the optimum opportunity for career development and remuneration for service
- to generate sufficient profit for growth and improvement to our business
- to ensure the constant maintenance of our high standards of quality control
- to maintain the best possible human relations with staff, customers and business associates
- to keep at the forefront of technological development and production techniques
- to maintain the training and technical standards of our engineering staff.

The statement will take time to develop and as much care as possible should be taken in producing it. At the end it should be:

- ✓ generally right (giving general direction, key values)
- ✓ enduring (not being changed every five minutes)
- ✓ succinct (key words, ideas)

✓ memorable (remembered for what it is)

✓ believable (credible)

✓ motivating (exciting, visionary).

THE KEY ELEMENTS IN THE MARKETING PLAN

Planning is, in effect, adapting your business strengths, acumen, staff resources and energy so that each will mutually support the other and then applying them to a coherent application for the future. Each of the many facets of your business will define its own strategy, particular to its interest, which in turn will be structured and fashioned into your overall business strategy. Marketing plays a crucial role in the process, by defining, analysing and shaping individual goals and objectives into programmes and plans. The marketing plan lies at the centre of a web of mutually supporting

Figure 4.1   The components of the marketing plan

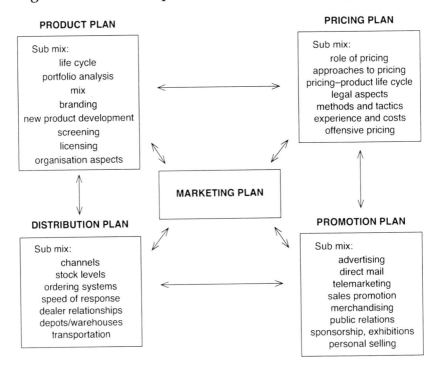

plans dealing with the components of the marketing mix. The planning process co-ordinates the salient points of each and summarises the result in the overall marketing plan as shown in Figure 4.1. In view of this each subsidiary plan will be examined in detail before we turn to the marketing plan itself.

THE PRODUCT PLAN

The policy governing the product will be a central pre-occupation of your marketing. There are two aspects: one is the management of your current range of products, the second, the development of new or modified products and services. Remember that a product is the whole bundle of things – product, information, service and other attributes – that provide a want-satisfying package which is bought for the benefit it provides to the customer and not necessarily for the features it offers. You should think in five levels, as shown in Figure 4.2.

Figure 4.2   The augmented product

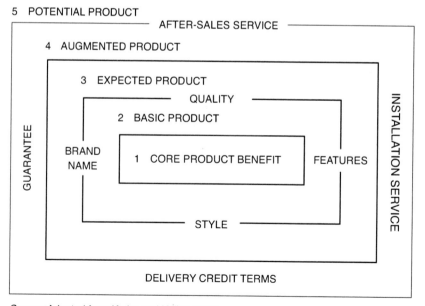

Source: Adapted from Kotler and Keller, 2006

At the centre there is the core benefit or service from the product. Surrounding it is the basic product and surrounding this is the expected product which you have prepared for the customer. These levels embrace tangible aspects, packaging, brand, quality, features. The fourth level is the augmented product, which is what can be added of value to the customer such as after-sales service, installation, delivery and guarantee. The final level is what the product might be if you combine the previous four levels with innovation and imagination, i.e. new ways to satisfy and delight your customers.

The product mix refers to the products sold by a business. Single products tend not to satisfy consumers and therefore a product line is developed containing a group of broadly similar products, aimed at a target group of consumers. The next stage is multiple product lines, which diversify your product range and the target consumer group. Branding has become a very strong feature of modern marketing and will confront you as you develop your marketing strategy. In reality businesses often divide into two types: branders or suppliers. Branders – Nike is a leading example – own and manage their brands. They design and specify the products and services, they control the research and development and own the technology. They manage the interface with the customer and end-user but do not actually make and manufacture the product. Suppliers, on the other hand, have no brands and focus on supply and operations. They are sub-contractors or process engineers and interface with the brander not the consumer. While both branders and suppliers may be profitable, the branders achieve much higher margins whereas suppliers are often threatened by competition because somebody somewhere in the world can provide the product or service cheaper than them.

Almost all products supplied to consumers today have some form of branding associated with them, ranging from signs to colours. Branding has certain advantages: it provides product protection, inspires brand loyalty and assists business image projection and advertising. Although there are potential disadvantages, the development of brand names enhances a product and helps to make it profitable. A brand name should say something about the product's benefits and qualities, be easy to pronounce, recognisable and distinctive.

New product development is an expression of the vitality of a business. Those which do not develop new products are exposed to risk from competitors and the markets. Products are vulnerable to change and have a finite life span and therefore new product development is almost a question of survival as a business tries to stay ahead and maintain profitability. Remember Edison's famous quote that inventiveness is 1% inspiration and 99% perspiration. Various organisational forms are suggested to handle new product development (NPD) but still the most tried and tested way to minimise risk and to enhance NPD is to follow a systematic process, create an effective organisation to handle this process and employ the best means at your disposal at each stage of development. The process is shown in Figure 4.3.

Having set out our strategic purpose this has to be translated into a product development strategy which reinforces the idea of a core benefit proposition that can be offered to the customer and which has value and competitive

Figure 4.3   The new product process – stage gate model

Business strategy
↓
New product strategy development
↓
Idea generation
↓
Screening and evaluation
↓
Business analysis
↓
Development
↓
Testing
↓
Commercialisation

superiority. The product development process can then be implemented, starting with the following:

Idea generation   Ideas can be developed from a variety of sources but there is conflict here between the need for creativity and the nature of your organisation which, to be efficient, will be focused on today's products and aiming to routinise and systemise what you do. To stimulate new ideas and new products requires creative people, an environment receptive to new ideas and the use of creative problem-solving techniques. Sources of ideas are many and varied: employees such as the sales force interface with the customer direct and hear at first hand complaints and requirements; service engineers are in contact with users and operators; and customer service personnel receive suggestions, complaints and criticisms regarding service and performance. Other sources may come from customers themselves, distributors, suppliers, competitors and others such as inventors, advertising agencies, designers and researchers. Alternatively, universities or independent agency laboratories may be potential sources. There is increasing evidence that the sources of ideas and methods of generating ideas have an effect on success rates for new products. While cause and effect are difficult to measure, established firms spend large amounts in an effort to find product winners.

Screening and evaluation   If a firm is successful in generating ideas, some means of evaluating their future worth is required. Various systems and techniques have been used and recommended but the key factors that have to be evaluated are:

- potential – market size and growth prospects
- penetration – the strength and vulnerability of competitors
- scale – market share and strength
- input – the investment required
- reward – profit margin and return on investment
- risk – the possibility of loss.

Business analysis Following the screening of ideas and prior to any large-scale investment, a feasibility study involving both commercial and technical evaluation should be undertaken.

Development The importance of this stage is that costs now begin to rise dramatically and this scale of input is matched with highly uncertain outcomes. To make a prototype or trial a service will incur premises, plant and equipment and in some cases may be as much as the cost of setting up full production or operational facilities.

Testing Even at this stage, indeed throughout the process, market evaluation needs to be undertaken to establish customer acceptance. Various ways can be used to test acceptability of both the product idea, prototypes and real products. Concept testing can evaluate the initial idea, product testing can be used to ensure the product works in the way intended and test marketing can assess the commercial viability prior to national or international launch. Although these evaluation measures involve additional expenditure they are crucial in reducing the costs and risk of failure and also ensuring that the product meets the customer's need in the way intended.

Commercialisation Eventually products which survive this process make it to launch stage. Adopting a marketing-led and customer-focused approach is essential for success. The platform for this success must be based on building a new customer base by creating value, outperforming the competition and differentiating the product in the mind of the customer.

Having gone through all these stages, there is no guarantee of market success. Many studies in the US and in Europe suggest that between 20% and 80% of new products fail in the consumer, service and industrial markets.

THE PRICING PLAN

Pricing is a difficult problem, which has to take into consideration many variables before a decision is reached. It is

Figure 4.4   The pricing process

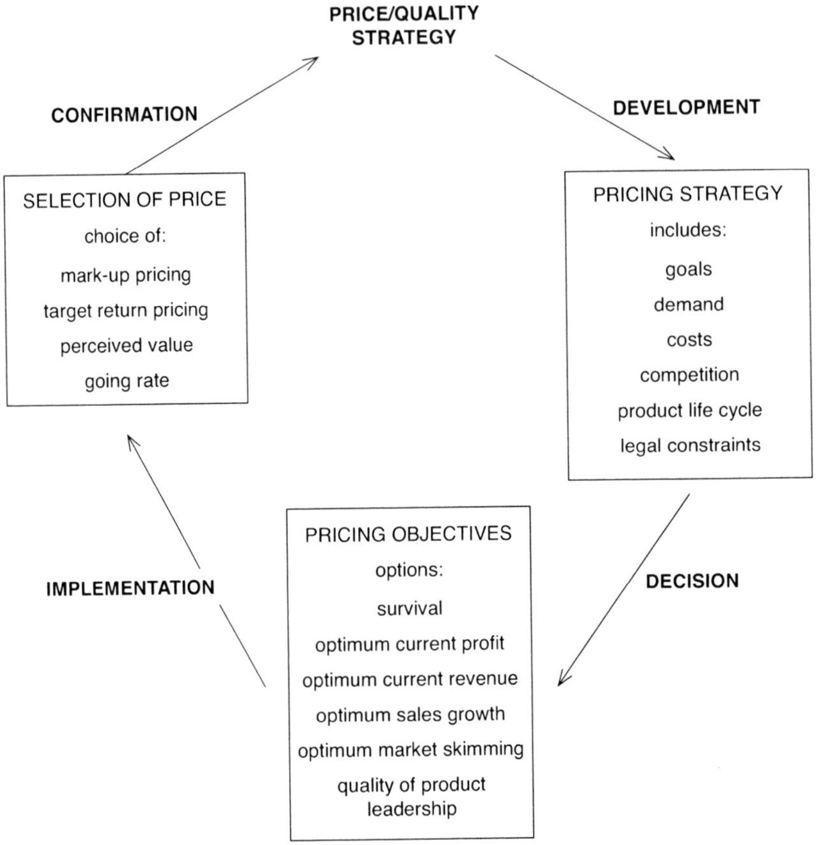

PRICE/QUALITY
STRATEGY

CONFIRMATION   DEVELOPMENT

SELECTION OF PRICE

choice of:

mark-up pricing

target return pricing

perceived value

going rate

PRICING STRATEGY

includes:

goals

demand

costs

competition

product life cycle

legal constraints

IMPLEMENTATION

PRICING OBJECTIVES

options:

survival

optimum current profit

optimum current revenue

optimum sales growth

optimum market skimming

quality of product
leadership

DECISION

particularly sensitive to market forces and is thus subject to constant scrutiny and adjustment by a business, to ensure that it meets aspirations and expectations. This section provides a sequential approach to the topic of pricing and presents it in a logical and progressive format.

The significance of price is that it is the only component of the marketing plan mix which generates revenue; all the others generate costs. Therefore the pricing of a product must be high enough to cover costs and make a profit, yet low enough to gain maximum benefit from demand and sales. It can be viewed as an entity, or as part of the overall pricing strategy of the business covering a range of products. In either case the effect of price competition from other businesses on yours needs to be taken into consideration. Your pricing plans must be flexible and responsive to market-related forces and carried out with discipline and judgement. The cycle of events governing a pricing plan is shown in Figure 4.4.

PRICING STRATEGY

At the outset, you have to decide in broad outline what the positioning of the product is in terms of its quality and price strategy. Price remains a key determining factor in consumer purchase and its combination with the quality of the product sets the scene for your business in its subsequent deliberations on pricing and business objectives. A typical combination of the quality/price mix essentially falls into a matrix of nine options, illustrated at Figure 4.5.

The price option you decide on should take account of the following explanation from the matrix. As shown in Figure 4.5, the diagonal squares 1, 5 and 9 represent a matching sequence in which quality is balanced with price and will give satisfaction to the target market. Squares 2, 3 and 6 are variations which can be adopted to improve or modify the diagonal positions. Square 2 offers a better deal at less cost than square 1, overtaken by square 3 which offers the best deal of all. The squares 4, 7 and 8 overprice the product

Figure 4.5   The product quality/price relationship

		PRICE		
		HIGH	MEDIUM	LOW
	HIGH	1. PREMIUM	2. HIGH VALUE	3. SUPERB VALUE
PRODUCT QUALITY	MEDIUM	4. OVERCHARGE	5. MEDIUM	6. GOOD VALUE
	LOW	7. EXPLOITATION	8. FALSE ECONOMY	9. ECONOMY

in comparison to its quality, a high-risk move which in all probability will backfire on your business, in the form of customer disenchantment and bad publicity.

PRICING OBJECTIVES

The progression from the pricing strategy to examining the principal pricing objectives governing pricing decisions is your next step in the development process. Each heading should encourage you to apply the basic principle to particular aspects of your business and help you formulate the necessary decisions. A business has to decide in general terms what it wishes to achieve with the product or product range in the market. Your selection of the target market and market positioning lead naturally into the marketing-mix strategy, which includes pricing. Pricing objectives must be set based on what it is you wish to achieve. In some cases your objectives will be limited by the circumstances in which you operate: for example, sealed bid pricing for a contract; or a variation, as in the case of geographic pricing, where the price is related to customer distance from the distribution point. The following six pricing objectives are those commonly applied in the running of a business.

Survival   This is a measure of desperation and is a short-term objective designed to keep a business going in face of difficulties. It implies reduced prices below costs, simply to maintain a cash flow.

Optimum current profit   This is a somewhat risky objective, in which a price is chosen to maximise the rate of return. Demand and costs are difficult to estimate and threats exist from competitor reaction and legal constraints on pricing.

Optimum current revenue   This is a more long-term objective with the intent to maximise sales revenue. It requires an estimate of the product demand and the energetic motivation of the sales force. There is a body of opinion that considers this method will lead to optimum profits and growth.

Optimum sales growth   This objective aims to increase the volume of sales, thereby lowering unit costs and raising long-term profits. The principal assumption is that the market is price-sensitive and that, as a consequence, lower than average prices will stimulate market growth and discourage competitors.

Optimum market skimming   This objective sets relatively high prices aimed at particular market segments, which can then be readjusted to lower levels to attract different and hopefully a greater number of market segments. It depends on a high demand, a lack of competitor interest and a high quality product image.

Quality product leadership   This objective aims at a high price for a high quality product and excellent after-sales service. Brand name association is probably the most important feature of this objective.

SETTING PRICE

In setting prices we need to take account of the following:

Demand   A basic law of economics is that as price falls demand increases and a firm should continue to increase output up to the point where marginal revenue is still positive. While this makes sense in a logical, abstract way, firms must take account of fluctuating and uncertain costs and the competition. There are many non-price effects on demand such as image and branding and, in particular, promotion. For most managers information is not always available in exact terms or quickly enough for rational and consistent pricing decisions. Nevertheless, it is helpful to have some idea of the demand curve for your product even if inexact. Particularly important is the concept of elasticity of demand, i.e. the responsiveness of demand to a change in price. Some products like cigarettes are relatively inelastic, at least in the short run. That is, as price rises demand is relatively unaffected. The degree of elasticity for your product is likely to be a function of the availability of close substitutes, price awareness by the consumer, habit or purchase inertia and the relative prices of other goods.

Different levels of demand are established by the range of price options you have available for selection. Pricing sensitivity and price elasticity are the keys to maintaining a grip on consumer demand.

A more sophisticated approach to demand-led pricing is perceived value pricing. The price is based on the perceived value of the product to the prospective buyer, and not the product's cost. It fits in well with product-positioning where a product is developed for a target market with a planned quality and price. It is the perception of the product value in the market which will determine success or failure.

Costs   Business costs are the foundation of any pricing plan. A private enterprise cannot operate if prices are set below costs or not for very long. Your business will wish to charge a price which will cover production and give a fair return. You will need to assess how costs can be varied with different levels of production and if costs can be lowered in proportion to production efficiency. Certainly account has to be taken of costs but whether it should be the basis for fixing price levels is less certain. One way to establish price is to use break-even analysis. This can be achieved as shown in Figure 4.6.

The break-even price is where all costs are covered by total revenue. By varying selling prices different break-even points occur. There are two particular problems with break-even analysis: first, the difficulty in establishing a sales forecast for different price levels; and, secondly, accurately estimating costs before prices are set. It is not really a technique for setting prices but one of assessing the effects of different price positions.

Another cost-based method of pricing is the mark-up method, typical in retailing. This is a very basic method of pricing in which a standard profit mark-up is added to the costs of production. It fails to take account of competitors or the nature of demand and is therefore limited in its application and may not achieve the best price for the product. Confusion sometimes arises depending on whether the cost price or selling price is used as the basis for the mark-up. For example,

Figure 4.6   The break-even chart

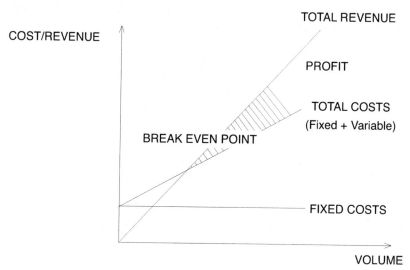

a product costing £1 selling for £1.25 has a mark-up of 25% on cost: 25p over £1 = 25%. The true margin is 25p over £1.25 = 20%.

Cost-plus pricing is the most well-known and widely used method of pricing. Although simple in principle, this method often disguises the fact that costs per item are sometimes difficult to measure accurately and for some products change rapidly. It is appropriate for working out a base or minimum price but the price established may be unrelated to demand and your competitors may not operate on the same cost basis. Remember that economies of scale, reduced learning costs and productivity will affect cost structures. A more common form of cost-plus is the concept of added value. This is particularly useful where fixed and variable costs are relatively stable yet the material component is less predictable:

$$\text{Added value} = \frac{\text{Selling price} - \text{Material costs}}{\text{Selling price}}$$

Another variation of cost-plus pricing is target return pricing. This pricing technique is based on setting prices to gain a target of return on investment. The problems of this procedure are broadly similar to mark-up pricing and much depends on price elasticity and the prices of competitors.

Competition   Another basis for pricing is to relate to the competition. Where products are undifferentiated and competitors many, it would be folly to charge premium prices unless factors such as image and service are important. Many markets are represented by acrimonious price wars, such as petrol and soft drinks. Generally, where a market does not value service, image or brand loyalty then suppliers will be unable to command a premium price. However, prices can often be established by the assessment of competitors' prices and offers. You may have to follow a market leader, in which case you will have little room for manoeuvre. On the other hand, if you hold an advantage, e.g. technological, manufacturing or marketing, this will allow you much greater flexibility in your pricing plan.

Going-rate pricing is one form of pricing based primarily on competitors' prices and, by charging basically the same rate with only minor variations, it maintains a status quo in the market and reduces the chance of a price war. It is quite a popular method, when costs are difficult to measure and competitor response is unclear.

Whatever method of pricing is chosen it should be part of your planning process and take account of other factors. One of these is the stage the product has reached in its life cycle. This is a recurring theme in the process of marketing. Products have a finite life and, through the various stages of their introduction, growth, maturity and decline, present continual pricing challenges. This is such an indeterminate process that only constant monitoring of their progress will enable you to adjust your pricing plan accordingly.

Another factor is legal constraints. This is a broad issue and covers not only business in the export market, but also domestic market considerations. Product subsidies, price legislation, anti-monopoly rules, price collusion and price manipulation are applicable to both considerations and need constant analysis and scrutiny. In addition, you need to pay attention to constraints on pricing, price promotion and retail price maintenance.

Finally, discounts. Most businesses can modify their basic price to entice or reward customers. Price adjustments, in the manner of discounts or allowances, come in a variety of forms. These range from the straightforward cash discount rewarding customers for prompt payment of bills, to discounts for quantity buying, functional discounts for business assistance, seasonal discounts for out-of-season buying and such things as trade-in and promotional allowances. Discounts will form part of the pricing structure decided upon and are indicative of the flexibility a good pricing plan can offer.

PRICE AS A MEANS OF PROFIT IMPROVEMENT

A firm can improve its profitability in one of three main ways:

- improve sales
- reduce costs
- increase prices.

The previous analysis suggests that price can range from a low, in which no profit will be realised, to a high which will not produce a demand. Between the two extremes there are three principal factors to be taken into account, namely product costs (which are the bottom line for pricing), prices of competitors and product substitutes (which provide a marker), and unique product features (which provide the justification for the price level decided upon). The diagram in Figure 4.7 summarises the points.

Figure 4.7 Setting a price

LOW PRICE	RANGE OF ACCEPTABLE PRICES	HIGH PRICE
No possible profit at this price.		No possible demand at this price

If price is chosen as the means of profit improvement this means a trade-off between low demand (price too high) and no profit (price too low). Price is often the favoured technique for improving profits for the following reasons:

- Nothing acts on a company's profits as quickly as a price increase which does not depress sales.

- Improving sales and reducing costs require much more time and effort to implement than does a price increase.

- Techniques for improving profits quickly in the short run are less effective than price increases.

- Sales improvements or cost reductions involve more than one department and necessitate co-ordinated action.

- Risk is higher in sales-increase policies and cost-reduction exercises may also be uncertain.

To show how effective price can be on profitability consider the following example (adapted from an idea by John Winkler). Assume a company has sales and cost structure as follows:

Sales	100
Variable costs	50
Overhead costs	40
Net profit	10

Using the three basic methods of profit improvement can produce the following result:

	+10% Sales	−12.5% Costs	+5% Price
Sales	110	100	105
Variable costs	55	50	50
Overhead costs	40	35	40
Profit	15	15	15

In any profit improvement exercise it is clear that a change in price has an overwhelming impact on net profit provided sales volume does not fall. At the same time the administrative burden is small and the return faster. There is still, of course, some risk since, other things being equal, as price increases demand will fall.

Another way to consider profit improvement is the cumulative effect of an increase in sales, a reduction in costs and a price increase. Using the same figures as previously, combining a 1% sales increase with a 1% cost saving and a 1% price increase results in a 24.5% profit increase.

		+1% Sales	−1% Costs	+1% Price
Sales	100	101	101	102
Variable costs	50	50.50	49.95	49.95
Overhead costs	40	40.00	39.60	39.60
Profit	10	10.50	11.45	12.45
				= 24.5% increase

With a number of markets experiencing zero or negative growth, firms have had to change the emphasis from sales expansion to conserving resources and improving efficiency. While product policy, innovation and marketing are all important, so too is price. Consumers seek value for money no matter at what end of our price spectrum the consumer is – high or low. Firms in static markets who face cost increases and attempt to combat competition with price increases face a difficult situation. Consider the problem of a sales reduction, cost increase and price reduction:

		-5% Sales	+5% Costs (inflation)	-5% Price (discount)
Sales	100	95.000	95.000	90.250
Variable costs	50	47.500	49.875	49.875
Overhead costs	40	40.000	42.000	42.000
Profit	10	7.500	3.125	(1.625)
Change in profit (%)		-25%	-69%	-116%

Many companies have made this mistake. A relatively small drop in sales at the same time as increasing costs is compounded by the mistake of trying to buy back sales volume in declining markets by giving away extra discounts. For these reasons a company should have a pricing plan which takes into account some or all of the following:

- the dominance of the firm's market position and its market share
- the degree to which substitute products are available
- the likelihood of competitive response
- the anticipated rise in costs
- the price elasticity of demand
- the company's long-term business objectives
- the effects of technology on future production costs
- the need for company growth in sales volume
- government restrictions, if any
- short-term profit needs, cash flow
- pricing impact on profits.

In summary, the complexity of pricing demands that you give great care and attention to its application. Pricing can be used in a variety of ways to enhance the conduct of a business, either as a tactical measure for the short term or as a part of a longer-term strategy. Its inherent flexibility to match competition and the effect of market forces makes it one of the most important factors in the marketing plan.

THE DISTRIBUTION PLAN

The third 'P', Place, is more properly termed distribution and channel management. Channel design and management is a major factor in the fulfilment of orders and is the process of managing the movement and storage of products from the manufacturer to the customer. In today's service and electronic world distribution is a rather anachronistic term for routes to market. Nevertheless, whether or not your business is directly involved in the mechanics of distribution, it is an important factor of marketing which will affect your business in some shape or form.

Distribution combines the physical movement aspect of distribution with the channels of distribution to accomplish its aim, as shown in Figure 4.8.

Figure 4.8   Routes to market

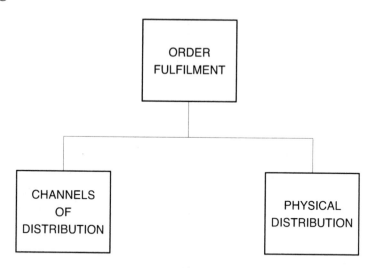

A key consideration in the channel strategy is the level of customer service and satisfaction a business wishes to aspire to. Getting the product to the right place at the right time, in sufficient quantity, requires careful analysis and monitoring of the various distribution options available. Almost every establishment that sells alcohol stocks a bottle of Guinness.

This is not the result of divine intervention or 'pure genius' but is achieved through a comprehensive distribution system linking two production outlets with millions of end-users. Bear in mind that even the perfect product, attractively priced and ingeniously promoted, cannot be sold without a means of distributing it to consumers. Again, one of the skills in marketing and one of the sources of comparative advantage for any business is the way in which control, co-operation and efficiency is achieved in distribution channel management.

A criticism often levelled by consumers is that the price of a product is high and the cost of distribution and the margins added by intermediaries inflate the price of products. In fact, although some distributors may have been slow to achieve cost savings and improve productivity compared with manufacturing units, distribution costs as a percentage of total cost have fallen from 17.4% in 1965 to 12.9% in 1985 and a staggering 4.5% in 2005. The Dell model of direct supply has revolutionised the personal PC market and radically altered the supply chain in that industry. In channel management the reason for the existence of intermediaries is that they add utility of place to the marketing of goods. Producers achieve economies through specialisation, i.e. large quantities of a small number of products, whereas consumers want small quantities of a large number and range of products.

There have been a number of factors that have led to changes and productivity improvements in distribution: first, the use of containerisation for the transportation of manufactured products; secondly, the use of information technology including electronic systems for ordering and inventory of products with widespread use of bar coding, electronic point of sale, telemetry and other forms of automation; and thirdly, changes in shopping practices, e.g. the growth of large shopping centres, shopping malls and the dominance of supermarkets. Improved response times for order and delivery have heightened the expectations of customers and you must consider how to capitalise on this to maintain and improve your customer satisfaction levels.

The choices facing your business in establishing distribution objectives are deceptively simple, but extremely important in that they can make or break customer relationships by the level of customer service they give. One is the direct distribution channel from seller to buyer, the other through distributors superimposed on this direct route. A list of options from a manufacturer's position is shown in Figure 4.9.

Figure 4.9   Distribution options

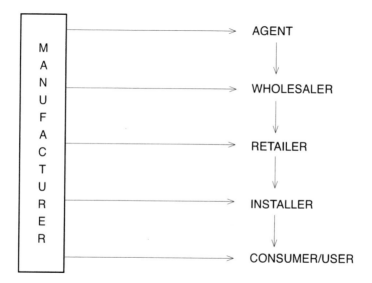

The link between producer and end-user can be dominated by the manufacturer or by the channel intermediary and this will depend on the degree of co-operation and control one party can exert upon the other. From a producer perspective they can operate within existing channels or attempt to create alternative ways to reach consumers. Direct Line insurance, Dell computers and IKEA furniture stores are three highly successful examples of taking a radical approach to the existing conventional distribution systems. Similarly, the physical distribution, including storage, stocking and transportation, can either come from the internal resources of the business or be contracted out. Your choice is dependent on the nature of the business and its particular objectives, e.g. reduction of costs, improved delivery times, logistic parameters of the product and service.

If the success or failure of distribution rests on customer service, distribution strategies have to be viewed from the perspective of the customer. A number of factors emerge from this viewpoint and should be considered in the selection of a distribution strategy which combines the institutional and functional aspects of distribution. These factors are:

- speed of response
- reliability and frequency of delivery
- availability of stock
- constraints on order size
- customer convenience / treatment
- complaints procedure
- order status information
- condition of goods on delivery
- invoicing procedures.

The order of importance in the list will be dictated by market research and maintain the focus of your business on the customer. Distribution costs are significant and work to the favour of the larger rather than the smaller business, which is why the analysis of costs and the selection of distribution choice is so important. You must study what the customer wants and what competitors are offering, and ultimately establish physical distribution objectives which are weighted in your favour. A comparative distribution audit on your business and your competitors is a valuable exercise, which will allow you to identify strengths and weaknesses and capitalise on them. Store checks, test ordering, governmental and business statistical sources and market research will all contribute to a comprehensive examination.

The gap between production and consumption has been referred to as the 'discrepancy of assortments' (Alderson, 1957) and these gaps are as follows:

- time gaps arising from firms producing continuously whereas consumers buy at discrete intervals either regular or irregular, sometimes involving lengthy periods of storage, e.g. garden equipment, fireworks;

- space gaps because producers are normally located in one or a few areas whereas consumers are widely spread;

- quantity gaps where firms produce in volume for economic reasons whereas consumers purchase in small quantities;

- variety gaps where producers make according to their resources and skills whereas consumers purchase to satisfy needs;

- information and communication gaps between producer, customer and end-user.

The decisions which have to be taken relate to both channel design and management. For example, some firms rely on their appeal with consumers to *pull* the product through distribution (e.g. Kelloggs, Black and Decker). Other firms adopt a *push* strategy by aiming to have the product available at the point of purchase. Specific decisions have to be made on:

- directness? How many levels from Figure 4.9 are to be used?

- number? Given each level, how many are to be used? The options are to use intensive coverage (as many as possible), selective (e.g. on a status or geographical basis) or exclusive (where only one distributor is used).

- types of middlemen? Whether to use agents who do not stock or deliver to full service distributors perhaps offering installation and design services.

- number of channels? It is possible to segment markets and perhaps use a variety of distribution options.

- degree of co-operation? This can be formal or informal, legal or flexible.

Channel management is about planning, organising and controlling the decisions made concerning channel design. Historically, most distribution channels were composed of small independent firms dealing with each other at arm's length. Separation like this can lead to inefficiencies and, as information needs increase, fluctuations in stock levels also increase. The result has been a need for closer links or what is called vertical marketing systems. These systems can be corporate where the ownership at different levels is by one firm, e.g. Laura Ashley or Avon cosmetics. To be viable the scale of operations needs to be large and efficient with obvious advantages in buying power and other economies of scale. An alternative system is the contractual one where there are voluntary chains such as SPAR and other retail co-operatives and franchises like McDonalds. Finally, looser forms of integration can be developed where one party tends to dominate the distribution system. These are administered systems, as used by Marks and Spencer.

The pressure of today's markets tends to favour retailers who not only sell products but buy on behalf of their customers. Other trends in distribution include:

- more attention to supplier's products by middlemen and retailers;
- more efficient coverage of areas whether geographic or by market segment;
- better information about end-users which can be processed more quickly and used speedily;
- reducing stock costs;
- improvement in delivery time, order processing and invoicing.

THE PROMOTION PLAN

Perhaps more misunderstanding occurs with the promotional aspects of marketing than any other. This is strange because promotion is the means by which an organisation communicates with its customers. Like most areas of business some communication is good, some bad, some professional, some amateurish, some legal and honest, some downright criminal. For our purposes we should understand the nature of communication and how to manage it effectively. The starting point is to understand the communication process, as shown in Figure 4.10.

Figure 4.10 A marketing communications model

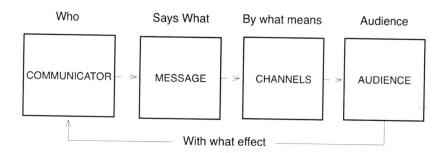

The idea of the model is that communication involves a feedback loop. In other words, communication is a two-way process. Again the author would claim that this process is most effective by adopting a planned approach to communications, particularly effective when integrated elements in promotion are combined consistently with other elements in the marketing mix. The four major elements of the promotional mix are advertising, sales promotion, public relations and personal selling. These elements must be tailored and integrated to communicate your business and its products to target customers. Each is different in its approach, but there is a fair degree of overlap in their application (Figure 4.11).

Advertising uses mass media, radio, press, TV, internet and other vehicles to reach a wide public audience. It also includes such things as exhibitions, trade shows, displays, direct mail and all forms of advertising literature. You need to provide an overall focus for advertising to build long-term sales and business/brand loyalty. Promotional advertising

Figure 4.11   The main elements of promotion

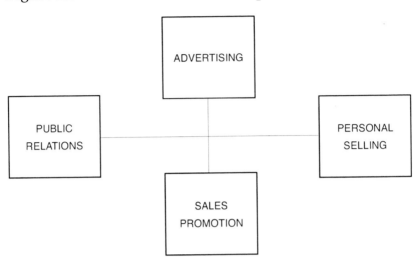

can emphasise features and benefits and vary according to the geographic application, i.e. local or national. It is a very public but impersonal form of one-way communication, which is very effective in reaching a geographically dispersed audience. The costs will vary depending on the medium chosen.

Sales promotion Sales promotion uses much the same media as advertising and has become a very powerful tool in the success of marketing planning. Sales promotion accounts for a considerable slice of advertising and uses a variety of ways to accomplish its aim. Included in your sales promotion will also be specific sales objectives. These are focused on the three main areas of the promotion field: consumers, trade and business.

Consumer promotion relies on short-term novelties to attract attention. The more common are free product samples, prizes, coupons, price packs, gifts, product warranty, cash refund offers and tie-in promotions. Price packs (i.e. two for the price of one), and coupons distributed through the mail or product packaging and newspapers, are two of the most effective methods in stimulating short-term sales. Tie-in promotions, in which two or more businesses team up to support each other, are also in vogue. You will have to bear in mind that the promotional measure you choose should have a sales generation value higher than the cost of the promotion.

Trade promotion has been estimated to be on a par with, if not larger than, consumer promotion. Manufacturers try to encourage wholesalers and retailers to carry their product in as great a volume as possible and to promote it strongly. The match is not entirely satisfactory, since many of the price-reduction measures, such as discounts and allowances, do not necessarily filter through to the consumer and the favoured status of manufacturers is not guaranteed.

Business promotion is chiefly concerned with conventions and shows. These events attract wide interest and representation and generate business, establish customer contacts and pro-vide a forum to merchandise products.

The development of the promotional programme is a matter for the individual business and must take account of the following factors: the incentive offer, duration, timing, promotion and distribution and how much money you want to expend on the budget. Pre-testing and evaluation are essential control measures and can be applied with relative ease.

The establishment of sales objectives is a complicated and most important element of your promotion plan. It is a projection of the level of sales to your target market and helps to determine the amount of advertising and the size of the sales force, in addition to production levels and the number of distribution channels. Sales objectives will obviously have a substantial impact on your business and must therefore be an accurate and attainable estimate of the market over the short term lasting about one year, to the longer term over a minimum period of three years.

There are a number of methods of establishing your objectives based on market trends and projections, market share and, of course, the need to cover planned expenses. The data gathered from your marketing analysis will provide the necessary basis for your decision. The crucial point of sales objectives are that they must be kept continuously under review and adjusted to match market fluctuations.

Public relations is a sometimes misunderstood subject. It is defined as a deliberate planned and sustained effort to establish and maintain mutual understanding between a business and the public. The overlap of interest between it and the other elements of promotion is readily apparent.

Personal selling is persuasive, personal communication by sales people employed by the business. It is a trained skill in prospecting for sales, face-to-face presentation and demonstration and bargaining negotiation. It depends a great deal on the mutual support of the other elements of the promotional plan. Personal selling has a number of strengths, if properly handled. A positive interactive relationship between seller and buyer can lead to long-term mutual trading loyalty and the cultivation of responsive attitudes to buyer preferences. A strong innovative programme should also take note of the need to reward the motivation and enthusiasm of sales staff.

Understanding the communication process helps to formulate achievable and measurable objectives for promotional programmes, with the proviso that, inevitably, these will be specific to the company and the market to be served. Advertising, for example, rarely sells product by itself but can be highly effective in creating awareness and interest. The buying process itself can be identified in discrete stages:

Figure 4.12   The buying process

Awareness

Interest

Desire

Action

Satisfaction

Advertising is particularly effective at stages 1 and 2. It follows that direct evaluation of promotion by sales results fails to fully understand what, for example, advertising can and can not do. Examples of realistic communication objectives are as follows:

- to create awareness of a company or product
- to create positive attitudes to a company/company's products
- to support channel of distribution or selling effort
- to sell the product directly, e.g. direct mail.

More specific objectives might include:

Aim (of communicator)	Desired response (from recipient)
Direct response	'Fill in coupon'
Seek information	'Request for literature or sales call'
To improve recall or reinforce message	'That reminds me'
To modify or reinforce attitudes	'Interesting', 'Really', 'I always knew I was right'

The promotion mix has to do the following:

- **Identify the target audience** Start with a clear audience in mind. Research needs, attitudes, preferences and any other characteristics. It is important to establish the current image of the business and its products from the beliefs, ideas and impressions held by the audience.

- **Determine the promotion objectives** Once the target audience has been defined, the desired response is naturally to make a purchase. However, purchase is at the end of a lengthy consumer decision-making process. You have to move your audience to a higher state of buyer-readiness through five stages: aware-ness of, knowledge of, liking for, preference for, and conviction in, your business and products.

- **Design the message** Your message should attract attention, develop interest and a wish to buy, cul-minating in a purchase. It will fall into four parts: the content, the structure, the format and the source. The message content can range through a number of human emotions in its particular appeal. A rational approach appeals to a consumer's self-interest (price, quality, performance). An emotional approach may apply humour, pride, even guilt. The challenge is to design a message which avoids extremes and produces the desired response. The message structure should present the case in a logical order and be conclusive. The message format has to attract attention by the use of visual images and colour. The message source must have credibility, whoever is going to do it. The use of celebrities is commonplace, but they require three further attributes: expertise, trustworthiness and likeableness.

- **Select the promotional channels** There are two principal types: personal and non-personal. Personal is direct communication on a face-to-face basis and can be very influential and carry great weight. Non-personal channels are without personal contact and stem mainly from the media.

- **Allocate the budget** Expenditure on promotion can be decided using one of four methods: the affordable method in which you spend as much as you think you can afford; the sales percentage method in which expenditure is a percentage of sales; the parity with competitors method in which you spend as much as your competitors; the objective and task method in which you identify tasks to accomplish marketing objectives and cost them. The first three, while convenient, are not recommended since they do not link the spend to specific objectives. The objective and task method suggests a series of stages, namely:

- set the marketing objectives
- decide how these will be achieved
- set specific advertising goals
- estimate the budget required.

The benefit of this approach is that it clarifies the purpose of any promotion, it is a planned approach, it relates to the marketing concept, it emphasises some aspect of superiority or competitive advantage and it permits measurement and evaluation.

- **Decide the promotion mix** The budget will be distributed among the four elements of promotion – remember advertising is only one element. You will have to decide which mix suits the business and the weight of importance you place on one or a number of the elements. Figure 4.13 compares advertising, direct mail and personal selling.

- **Measure the results** The measurement of promotional effectiveness is difficult to assess with any degree of accuracy. Research, customer surveys and sales data will all contribute to a general indication.

- **Manage and co-ordinate the process** The promotion plan needs constant monitoring to ensure that the promotional direction and balance is right and that you are getting value for money.

The question of whether or not promotion pays can only be affirmative. The choice of media depends on finding the most cost-effective way to deliver the desired number of exposures to the target audience. The effect of any communication depends on reach (how many), frequency (how often) and impact (what effect). This is a highly complex decision and the following list details the plus and minus factors of various forms of media:

- **Television** Plus factors: audio-visual, immediate impact, extensive homogenous coverage, frequency.

  Minus factors: expensive, constraints of commercial transmissions.

Table 4.1   Personal selling, direct marketing and advertising compared

Personal selling	Direct mail	Advertising
Directed at the individual	Directed at the individual	Directed at a mass audience
Personal, direct contact	Impersonal, direct contact	Impersonal, indirect contact
High level of adaptability	Medium level of adaptability	Less directly adaptable
Working in depth	More broad than deep	Working in breadth
Two-way	One-way	One-way
Direct feedback	No voluntary feedback	Organised feedback
Expensive per contact	Very cheap per contact	Relatively cheap per contact
Push effect	Push effect	Pull effect

- **Radio**

  Plus factors: good medium for message frequency, good local/national coverage.

  Minus factors: audio impact only, commercial time constraints, 'hit or miss' reach.

- **Newspapers**

  Plus factors: immediate impact, potentially high reach, promotional assist (coupons).

  Minus factors: low number of readers per copy, short attention span, visual impact only.

- **Magazines/ trade publications**

  Plus factors: good quality, product description potential, audience potential, promotional assist (coupons), pass along readership.

  Minus factors: visual impact only, lower readership than newspapers.

- **Direct mail**   Plus factors: extensive coverage potential, good coupon carrier, contents and timing flexibility, selective message.
Minus factors: visual impact only, easily discarded, commonplace.

The use of media can be divided into two parts: planning and execution. The goal is to deliver the optimum number of messages to your target audience at the lowest cost in the most suitable environment. If at all possible you should try to arrange a combination of various media to fulfil your requirements. The planning will be dictated above all else by your budget and it is important that it should be detailed and thorough. You will have to analyse your product in relation to the market, your competitors' performance, awareness levels, attitudes and behaviour, and relate all of these to your sales objectives. In turn this will bring you to whom the message is being directed, the geographic destination and the timing and volume of the message transmission.

Whatever programme is decided it is important to assess its effect, take corrective action if appropriate and decide your future plans. Although the total effect of the promotional programme may be difficult to assess ('I know half my advertising is wasted but I don't know which half'), there are many specific techniques to assess individual elements (e.g. pre- and post-awareness levels before and after an advertising campaign). Various measures of recognition can also be used to assess how many saw, noted, believed and retained various communication messages. Professional management will set clear objectives, use whatever means they can to assess the impact of their efforts and take appropriate corrective action.

Having considered the elements of the marketing mix to invest in our marketing plan, we are now ready to prepare such a plan. To review our position, we can say that adoption of the marketing concept by a single business unit requires that the marketing plan reflects the correct emphasis on the individual elements of the marketing mix in response to customer requirements, in the most efficient manner, in a more effective way than competitors and in response to company objectives. These mix elements, both individually and together, have an effect on the internal operations of a company and are enhanced or negated by various external forces which may be hostile or benign.

THE MARKETING PLAN

The marketing plan incorporates the findings of the subsidiary plans, the marketing audit and analyses. It uses the information to project a strategic view of the future development of your business. It is formatted in a number of sections, titled as follows.

- Section 1.   The Executive Summary
- Section 2.   Current Marketing Situation
- Section 3.   Opportunities and Threats Analysis
- Section 4.   Strengths and Weaknesses Analysis
- Section 5.   Objectives
- Section 6.   Marketing Strategy
- Section 7.   Action Programme
- Section 8.   Projected Profit/Loss Statement
- Section 9.   Controls.

The Executive Summary is a brief extract of the principal findings, goals and recommendations from the main body of the plan. It provides senior managers with a fast, precise means of acquainting themselves with the important issues and great care must be taken to ensure it is complete and accurate.

The Current Marketing Situation will present information and statistical data from the marketing audit and the specialist analyses, in an overview of the current position of your business. It will contain data on:

- the size and growth of the market
- customer needs and perceptions of the product, purchase trends, etc

- sales, prices, profit margins
- competition size, goals, market share, products, intentions
- distribution, dealers, channels
- macro-environment, demography, technology, economy.

The Opportunities and Threats Analysis will take a comparative look at the major points raised in the SWOT analysis and decide on the way to minimise the effect of the threats and gain the maximum from the opportunities.

Objectives will be derived from the information gained so far and will fall into two categories: financial and marketing. These objectives will form the basis for subsequent strategies and action plans. The financial objectives are decided first, e.g. a net profit of a certain amount will be translated into an objective of a certain quantity of sales, and so on. Marketing objectives should be clearly stated and given a timeframe of accomplishment. They must be consistent with the overall aims and strategies of your business and if possible placed in an order of mutually supporting priority.

The Marketing Strategy determines the direction of your business. The achievement of marketing objectives will offer a number of choices. The selection of the choice will in its turn decide your marketing strategy. This process should not be conducted in isolation and wide-ranging discussion is recommended with other key persons in your business, e.g. finance (available funds), purchasing (provision of material, production levels), sales managers (sales force support).

The strategy should be disseminated as widely as possible within the business and a written statement is often best for precision and clarity. The contents will include such items as shown in Table 4.2.

Table 4.2   Strategy statement

Item	Example
Target market	Middle income family, male emphasis
Position	High quality, reliable DVD recorder
Product line	Two models, one lower price, less options
Price	Less than competitors
Distribution outlets	Principally chain radio/TV stores
Sales force	Expand staff
Service	High quality, responsive service
Advertising	New campaign, increase budget, emphasis on national media
Sales promotion	Increase budget, participate in displays and shows
Research and	Develop improvement/update programme development
Marketing research	Monitor competitors, improve consumer feedback on product

The Action Programme will centre on consumer and sales promotion and address the following questions:

- What is to be done?
- Who will do it?
- When will it be done?
- How much will it cost?

The Projected Profit/Loss Statement will summarise the forecasted financial impact of the plan and is essentially a balance between the forecast of the financial objectives and the cost of the action programmes.

Income	Expenditure
Forecast sales volume	Cost of production
Price	Distribution
	Marketing/sales

Controls form the final part of the plan. They monitor progress and developments and should be reviewed on a periodic basis to examine the current and future position of the plan as to whether fine-tuning or remedial action is required on potential difficulties. There are four principal control factors:

- control of the plan
- control of profitability
- control of efficiency
- control of strategy.

Plan control examines the performance of the plan in comparison to its stated goals. Any discrepancy between the two should be determined and corrected. The performance of the plan is measured against the following considerations:

Table 4.3   Control of the plan

Sales analysis.	Actual sales compared to projected sales.
Sales relative-to-competitors analysis.	Your market share against that of competitors. competitors.
Expenses-to-sales analysis.	The ratio of marketing expenses to sales.
Financial analysis.	Is your business making money? Profit margins, return on assets, etc.
Customer attitudes.	Monitor surveys, complaints and suggestion schemes, customer opinion panels.

Profitability control is a profit and loss measurement of products, business departments, customer relationships and distribution channels.

Efficiency control examines sales force efficiency, advertising efficiency, sales promotion efficiency and distribution efficiency.

Strategy control is the overall assessment in conjunction with the marketing audit.

The process of marketing planning should be designed to get the results you want in the customer market. A written marketing plan is a foundation document, giving a long-term view of your business in all the elements of marketing. It is fundamental to the motivation and direction of staff and the future development of your business. It should be accessible to all concerned and provide managers with the guidance and information they need to be responsive to business aims and goals and market changes.

5 SERVICE, QUALITY AND RELATIONSHIPS

There are three types of business person; those who make things happen, those who watch things happen, those who wonder what happened

Anonymous

CUSTOMER SERVICE

The expectation of higher standards of service is already a feature of the current market place and you could hardly be blamed for assuming that, if you offer the best possible service, you will prosper. However, customer expectations are continually rising and the levels to which they rise become the minimum levels customers expect; and thus differentiation between you and your competitors will become less clear.

A further consideration is that service has to be viewed from the point of view of the customer. Unless the customer values the service you offer, it is unlikely to gain the business you want. Therefore an early understanding of what really matters to a customer becomes a matter of priority. Customer judgement is notoriously fickle and can be very unfair. A case in point is the often-quoted airline example in which minor failures in cabin staff service to airline passengers become translated into a lack of flight safety. Nevertheless, such a situation has to be treated seriously because in the final analysis you want the business and it is the customer who pays.

The level of service you establish has to convince customers in its quality. There is no point in claiming a first-rate service when it fails to meet such a standard. Customers will feel cheated and the repercussions on your business will be severe. You must develop a consistent approach to service which matches the other aspects of your marketing plan, particularly price, but also the appropriate service quality needs of target customers, and maintain the ability to deliver to the required standards. A comparative examination of the performance of your competitors is a useful form of measurement.

Customer service is a long-standing issue, which has not been viewed with the same importance as it is in the present day. There are six principles in managing customer service:

- define the elements of service
- determine the customer's viewpoint
- design a competitive service package
- develop a programme to sell the service
- market test the service programme
- establish performance controls.

EMPOWERMENT

In essence you will have to think of the people who deliver service and the people who receive it. Staff training programmes in customer service, which motivate personnel to create a high standard of quality, also bring us to the subject of empowerment. Empowerment gives employees, outside the executive levels of a business, the authority to correct problems for customers as they occur. It is an excellent system for allowing employees to use their initiative, making them feel they are much more part of the organisation, and most important of all, enabling them to deal with problems as quickly and efficiently as possible, nipping them in the bud.

There is a high failure rate in customer service programmes, which indicates that business management may not be as serious in its approach to this vital concern as it should be. Customer service is an ethos which should run through your business from top to bottom. It requires more than lip-service to be of benefit and should be approached with commitment and training.

CUSTOMER SATISFACTION

There is general agreement that customer satisfaction is the goal of marketing, resulting in long-term customer loyalty and hence profit. It is no accident that a business with a high commitment to customer satisfaction will enjoy better profitability. The measurement and management of customer satisfaction is therefore a matter of considerable importance. You should start by identifying your customer base in as much detail as possible. The measurement aspect can be done very simply by using questionnaires, telephone surveys and freephone responses, supported by the personal approach by staff to customers, asking what they think of the business. It will also help to defuse often the most trivial situations and issues which create dissatisfaction among customers and is a most effective way of dealing with such problems. It is also helpful for your business to set and monitor standards for service, which will provide a measurement for customers to gauge their satisfaction. But perhaps the most important factor is listening to and learning from your customers.

The management of customer satisfaction stems in large part from the measurements you have taken. It puts right major criticisms and sensitive issues and must be positive in its application. It must be designed to keep customers coming back and match or exceed their expectations. Customer complaint procedures are a major component of this management. Customers must be invited to comment and their complaints investigated thoroughly. The procedure must be user-friendly and followed up by staff on an individual basis.

Customer service must never be taken for granted. It requires constant attention and supervision. The measurement analysis must be used to improve and put right customer service procedures and be continuously monitored. Customer service permeates all levels of a business and is a collective responsibility. There are several useful diagnostic exercises that can be used as a means of measuring your business approach to customer service and Figure 5.1 provides a useful first analysis.

Figure 5.1   Customer service and satisfaction assessment tool

Business: Market/Segment/Customer Type

Completed by: Date:

	How good are we at the following?	Remarks	Marks out of 10
1.	Measuring customer satisfaction	Doing it, being seen to do it, positively, systematically, routinely	
2.	Using customer satisfaction measurement to change our marketing policies	Whether we are seen and appreciated in our response	
3.	Using customer satisfaction measurement to evaluate and reward staff at all levels	Positive approach to measures	
4.	Ensuring all staff understand our strategy on customer service and quality	Not only telling, getting agreement and commitment Listening to what they say	
5.	Setting staff measurable goals for customer service and quality and evaluating performance	Follow-up performance Reaction to customer complaints, lost accounts, orders switched to competitors, unfavourable comments on performance	
6.	Consulting staff about customer needs, expectations, complaints Taking notice of staff comments	Respond to what staff say	
7.	Working together to remove obstacles and barriers to quality and service delivery to customers	Changing company rules and policies	
8.	Regularly evaluating our competitors' service and quality provision	Effect on sales, market share, customer loyalty, profitability	
9.	Having a clear and actionable service and quality strategy, compared to our competitors	Capable of consistent delivery and giving a clear position over our competitors	
	Conclusions / Implications / Actions		

Source: Adapted from Piercy, 1991

QUALITY

The demand for quality has made it one of the twin prongs of modern marketing. Quality and price now represent the most powerful influences affecting a customer's wish to obtain goods or services. The emergence of quality has occurred as a result of two features: a more demanding and discerning customer, faced with a wide range of products to choose from; and, more significantly, from the establishment of quality assurance and measurable, identifiable standards of quality.

Quality assurance is one of the first principles of marketing. It covers the spectrum of the product and marketing management operations and demands constant assessment and periodic review. It should aim at the prevention and elimination of problems associated with quality, underpinned by an effective system of documentation which can record all actions and activities. Quality assurance embraces the way you conduct your business, how your staff function, all aspects of the product or service you offer and external customer perception of the whole. The key factors in setting you on the road to effective quality assurance are good communications and quality management.

Good communications are essential to encourage the flow of information necessary for you to establish, maintain and improve quality. Communications encourage people to talk and make their views known and are particularly important in overcoming apathy and dissatisfaction. There is an internal and external dimension to communications in relation to quality. The nature of modern business does not lend itself to the free exchange of information and staff discussion. Businesses are complex and compartmented and there is as much difficulty in passing information as there is in receiving it. If your business is to gain the maximum benefit from the standards of quality you set, you must establish mechanisms, such as staff newsletters and staff meetings, within your business to ensure that regular communications are developed and maintained throughout each level. Let everyone know what is going on and encourage participation.

The external dimension of communications focuses on customer feedback and market research and provides a counter-balance to the question of internal communications. In order to meet the requirements of customers, you have to know how they feel and what they are looking for, in relation to your business and its products. There is a wealth of information available, which can be turned to your advantage, from customer surveys to the analysis of complaints. The collection of this information helps you to keep in touch with the customer and, by doing so, will establish a database of knowledge, which will be of significant benefit in your search for quality. External communications must not overlook the human factor in the staff–customer relationship. This critical interface is sometimes overshadowed by more esoteric marketing practices, but remains a most important element in the customer perception of the quality you offer. The receptionist, telephonist and shop assistant can make or break a business relationship, regardless of product. It is therefore in the management of quality that your quest lies.

Total Quality Management (TQM) has been a major innovation in business. It has moved out of the realm of manufacture and production and now encompasses customer values and how much a customer will pay for quality. TQM is based on the maintenance and continuous improvement of standards. It should be inserted into a product, programme or business procedures as a matter of course, rather than controlling bad quality out. It should eliminate waste, enhance product performance and, above all, improve customer satisfaction. TQM has to be managed properly and constantly keep the needs of customers in its sight.

It is the function of marketing to provide the lead and co-ordinate the various facets of TQM, such as product features, customer requirements, market review and positioning. These must then be interlinked to business objectives, techniques and attitudes and the motivation and training of staff. Having addressed the mechanisms and procedures, it is now a question of judging the effectiveness of TQM.

For those who simply wish to offer quality to the customer, a continuous assessment, which monitors and tests procedures and techniques, will ensure that quality remains in strong focus and that positive action can resolve any problem areas which come to light. Business performance, the training of staff, customer relations, product quality, are all taken into account and recorded to give continuity and consistency to the process.

Those who wish to achieve a more formal measurement of their quality standards will take advantage of the services of the Marketing Quality Assurance (MQA) certification process (http://www.mqa-ltd.co.uk). This is conducted by an accredited third party organisation, which specialises in the formal assessment of the quality control systems developed by a business for marketing, sales and customer services. This assessment is conducted to the Quality System Standards of the International Standards Organisation (ISO) 9001:2000 series, which incorporates the British Standard (BS) 5750, dealing with the same subject.

The standards incorporate a number of good management practices, which should be common practice within business, such as controls and inspections at each stage of production and delivery, through to purchase and after-sales service, training, audits and records, sampling procedures, reliability and an acceptance of responsibility. The MQA specification lists a number of requirements, categorised under 15 headings, which include such items as the existence of business plans; marketing and sales plans and operations; customer assurance issues; organisational and personnel issues; and all aspects of quality. If businesses achieve the required standard, MQA will award a certificate and the right to use the MQA mark. This award signifies, to employees and customers alike, that the business has gained an independent, professional recognition of its marketing capabilities and a visible factor of influence over its competitors.

The environment has become a factor of great importance in marketing and there is continuing sustained pressure on businesses to demonstrate their environmental policy and their support for environmental issues of the day. The approach clearly needed to be structured as a management system similar to quality assurance. As a result, BS 7750 was prepared a few years ago under the direction of the Environment and Pollution Standards Policy Committee, designed for any organisation to establish a management system for effective adherence to environment issues and audit of performance. The management principles of BS 7750 are shared in very large measure by those of BS 5750. Therefore the implementation of one will result to a great extent in matching the requirements of the other and provide considerable encouragement to complete both. These standards are currently being revised.

The focus on the customer in modern marketing has also raised the profile of quality as a major factor of influence in the marketing process. The guarantee of quality is underwritten by applying and meeting quality assurance standards. These standards produce tangible proof to the customer that a business and its products represent the best possible deal for their money and establish a measure of trust to encourage return custom. The benefits from raising the profile of quality within your business should therefore be self-evident.

BUSINESS RELATIONSHIPS

An emerging issue in business today is the importance of relationships and, in particular, the relationship between the firm as supplier and the customer or consumer. Initially this was seen as a sub-set of marketing and embraced database management, direct marketing techniques and customer relationship mechanisms. This has been most noticeable in business to consumer markets, especially services and financial services. Many schemes, although not all, are little more than sophisticated selling. More developed programmes explore new ways to view customers and seek a single view of the customer in order to manage relationships more effectively. This is the essence of marketing in practice and the key question is 'What can I do for you, Mr or Mrs customer, to gain more of your business?' In the relationship world, sellers do not have full control from design to delivery over the systems in a relationship environment. Advice on customer management systems often implies that customers are passive or only involved through use of the system. It has been our intention in this book to demonstrate the impact that marketing has in this prime relationship by understanding, involving and participating with the customer to achieve mutual satisfaction.

From the supplier perspective, a fundamental question for any business must concern the basis of its relationship with different role partners, especially buyers. Firms must choose the type of relationship appropriate to the product and market conditions in which they conduct their operations. Some buyer–seller relationships depend on technical performance and one party may be locked into a relationship, voluntarily or otherwise, due to technical dependency. Increasingly, customers can choose between technical options offering similar solutions. However, relationships can also be built on the functional aspects of a product or service. This entails how the service is delivered, the degree of support that is employed to enhance customer value and the effectiveness of the supply chain in meeting end-user requirements.

How a product or service is supplied in a relationship context involves considering the customer as an asset and therefore they become involved in the company's offering. The way companies manipulate their sales and service system impacts on relationships. Credibility and customer bonding can be lost or enhanced at the point of sale or indeed in how we communicate. However, bear in mind that relationships may depend also on the distinction between whether the product/service is purchased as a transaction or whether repeat business is the objective and a relationship should be nurtured and pursued. In the author's research, and in the companies he has worked with, hee found that, in most cases, product quality and service quality should be combined to establish and maintain a strategic market position. In business to business exchange processes, strategy can be formulated by considering the behaviour of individual accounts over time rather than customers being members of markets or market segments. This is not always the case in the business to consumer world.

Most large firms, to be effective, need to act like a small firm. This means being in touch with customers, responsive, flexible and adaptable. Most small firms, to be efficient, need to achieve some of the economies enjoyed by large firms. This means lower purchasing costs, economies in scale for advertising and selling and cash resources to fund their plans for development and expansion. This is the modern business paradox. The author's advocacy of a new order in management, based on understanding of the customer, is in part a response to the inability of large organisations to do what small firms must practice in order to survive: that is, keep in touch with customers, respond to the trends in the market and, in particular, to the changing demands of customers. Relationships can also provide a way for small firms to mobilise the resources enjoyed by large firms. In practice there is a gap between what firms do, what they should do and what is most desirable for any particular firm to do for any given market or group of customers at any particular point of time in their development.

6 FROM LOCAL TO GLOBAL

No nation was ever ruined by trade

Benjamin Franklin

Meeting the needs of any market or market segment can be daunting but as a firm moves into international markets it faces additional challenges. In today's complex world it may be that a firm has international customers from day one, although for pedagogical simplicity we will assume a firm already in existence is intending to operate in or sell to new overseas markets. Marketing in another country means the business has to cope with many different issues, such as culture, legal systems, currencies and documentation requirements. It will have to decide whether to use agents and distributors as its method of selling in foreign markets. Agents and distributors already have a sales organisation, understand the local culture and can be a more cost-effective means of market development than is establishing a sales subsidiary.

International marketing is littered with examples of firms that made expensive mistakes simply because they did not take the time to understand the market they were dealing with. In this chapter, we argue that taking time to assess the market and plan market entry and development will improve the chances of success. The international marketing environment is undergoing profound and rapid change. In most industries today, competition is becoming fiercer as more firms enter international markets and access to markets becomes easier. Even if a firm does not sell abroad, it is likely that it faces more competition from foreign firms in the home market and its domestic competitors may, by selling abroad, become more competitive in the home market.

CULTURAL DIFFERENCES

To compete globally, an understanding of the international marketing environment is vital, one of the key elements of the environment being the multiplicity of cultures that firms sell in. Culture underlies all our relationships in international marketing. It shapes the beliefs or standards of groups and helps individuals to decide what are appropriate behaviours and actions. One aspect of this is the existence of national or regional styles of doing business and conducting negotiations. For example, it is commonly held that there are typically Middle Eastern, Japanese, American and British ways of doing business. To demonstrate how radically different two negotiation styles can be, there follows a description of Middle Eastern and American negotiation styles. In describing the basic characteristics of a Middle Eastern style, it must be borne in mind that almost all countries in this category are Arab–Islamic, yet other religious groups, notably Christian minorities, are found throughout the region. Thus the assumption that this region is entirely Arab–Islamic is not the case but the characteristics of Arab–Islamic culture are as follows:

- Knowledge of the sub-group to which the negotiator belongs is essential; the relationships between the parties must be explored with great care, to find out who is who and what relationship each negotiator has with the different groups.

- The role of intermediaries ('sponsors' in Saudi Arabia) is very important. As a result of European colonisation over the last two centuries, the majority of 'middle Eastern' business people speak French or English and understand European civilisation; whereas the reverse is rarely true. Intermediaries must be employed for a simple reason: we (the Europeans and Americans) systematically underestimate the cultural divide.

- It must always be borne in mind that Middle Eastern civilisations were largely the founders of those in Europe. They have left many traces behind and, as far as art and culture are concerned, their influences were dominant for many centuries during the Middle Ages.

The pride of the person with whom you are dealing must be – truly – respected.

- One must expect a great deal of emotion, theatricality and demonstrativeness, interspersed with true pragmatism. The mixture is often bewildering. Friendship is sought, relationships are personalised, and the idea of a cold 'business-like' relationship is difficult to envisage. Once a true friend has been made (which is far from straightforward), the sense of loyalty can be very strong.

- When loans and interest are discussed it is best to be very cautious as interest or riba is forbidden by the Koran. There are acceptable forms of finance for business but the subject should be handled sensitively.

In contrast, the American style of negotiations is characterised by the following:

- A recognition that in conducting business negotiations the selection of negotiators and the preparation for talks is methodical.

- There is a tendency not to take sufficient account of the culture of other parties; a belief that the American way of doing business is the best way and other nationalities would benefit by adopting this way of doing business.

- Emphasis is placed on issues, facts and evidence in negotiation and the need to reach agreement by certain deadlines. Others groups, like the French, have a generally less timely sense of negotiations and debate more general principles relating to the negotiation, which could be interpreted as delaying tactics by Americans and may lead to resentment.

- Americans value frankness and sincerity, although being overly frank could in the extreme be construed as arrogance in cultures which have a more restricted view of self-assertion.

- A 'win' mentality where there is little sympathy for a loser, and business negotiations which may be conducted on the basis of may the 'best man win'.

- A recognition that contracts should be drawn up carefully and precisely in law and that these can be the basis of legal action if disputes arise in the future. American is a litigious nation.

- A tendency to be short-term oriented with an emphasis on getting results quickly. This can be a disadvantage in negotiations.

There are clearly major differences in the negotiating style of the Arab–Islamic and American cultures which can lead to misunderstandings and failed negotiations. It is not the case that every member of the Arab–Islamic or American cultures exhibits all of the characteristics attributed to the cultures above, but as a group the negotiating styles are recognisable and are characteristics of their respective business groups.

The key issue in discussing culture is to understand that culture is an important part of international business and has tangible effects on negotiations. When doing business in international markets, it is important to take the time to find out about the culture and styles of negotiation before going into a market, so that the likelihood of mistakes and misunderstandings is reduced. Government export promotion agencies publish information on doing business in foreign markets, and talks with export promotion officials, chambers of commerce and businessmen, who have knowledge of particular markets, is a good starting point for understanding and working in a different culture.

GLOBALISATION

Globalisation has become a key issue as a number of factors change the way in which companies – mainly multinational corporations but also smaller firms – organise and carry out their business activities. Firms can now identify and sell to similar market segments around the world and have developed global marketing strategies to exploit these markets. Multinational corporations have gradually changed from conducting business on a country-by-country basis to conducting business on a regional or global basis. This is done to achieve cost savings arising from increased economies of scale and from reducing the duplication of activities in markets. Although this is more difficult for a small business the information technology revolution enables firms to co-ordinate and control operations on a global basis that hitherto would have been impossible. Communication within organisations and externally with customers and suppliers is now quicker and more informative with the advent of improved international telecommunications and the internet.

The internet offers new capabilities for exchange in international markets and firms are developing strategies for the use of the internet to support their international marketing. The ease of communication between the exporter, customers and intermediaries will improve levels of customer service, with response to customer queries being faster. The provision of a website is feasible for any company and the internet can be used to search for customer prospects, to provide information and to transact.

The vast array of marketing-related information on the world wide web (www) provides an excellent tool for international research. Examples of directories and databases that list importers, exporters, distributors, wholesalers and agents are:

- Trade Research and Data Exchange
  (http://www.tradeinfo.com)
- Wholesalers Worldwide Marketplace
  (http://www.inetbiz.com/market/)
- Asia Pacific Manufacturers and Traders
  (http://apple.ia.com.hk/jk/jk.html)
- EUROPAGES (http://europages.com/); this is a purchaser's guide to 150,000 companies in more than 25 countries
- World Importers Directory
  (http://teleron.com/buyersguide.html)
- Serna International Import/Export Directory
  (http://www.cris.com/~serrany</start.shtml).

There are also many organisations offering trade lead services. IMEX Exchange (http://www.imex.com) offers firms access to many of the trade lead systems. Other useful sites include:

- Business City (http://www.businesscity.com/doc/Gtrade.htm)
- Tradebase (http://www.ita.doc.gov/industry/opec/ttools.htm)
- Trade Zone (http://www.tradezone.com/tz/trdzone.htm)
- Tradescope (http://www.owens.com/tradescp/tradeld.html).

From a political and economic standpoint, access to many markets is becoming easier with the increasing integration of markets. The European Union is dismantling barriers between member states and there has been a general reduction in barriers to trade, partly owing to the work of the World Trade Organisation (WTO), formerly GATT. For example, under the auspices of the WTO many countries have signed an agreement to eliminate almost all tariffs currently levied on information technology products.

AGENCY LAWS IN THE EUROPEAN UNION

Legal and regulatory systems also have a direct bearing on selling in international markets. For example, EU agency law, in the form of the Commercial Agents Directive, has widespread implications for firms selling in the European Union. The main points of the Commercial Agents Directive are summarised as follows:

- The Directive applies only to agents who operate in connection with the sale of goods and only within EU countries. Distributors who buy goods and then resell them on their own account are not covered.
- Where there is no agreement between parties, the agent will be entitled to remuneration that commercial agents 'are customarily allowed in the place where he carries on his activities'.

- Agents are entitled to commission on transactions completed, not only during the course of the agency contract but also afterwards if the transactions have been mainly attributable to their efforts.

- Agents must be supplied with a statement of commission due and the agent has the right to ask to see an extract from the principal's books.

- Where an agency contract is entered into for an indefinite period, each party is given a right to terminate it on notice. This provision may not be varied. The period of notice is one month during the first year of the contract, two months during the second year and three months thereafter.

- Agents are entitled to compensation for the damage they suffer when a contract is terminated.

- Compensation is not paid where the agent is in substantial breach of contract, nor if the agent terminates the contract, except where that termination is due to age or illness of the agent or due to facts attributable to the principal. There is no entitlement to compensation where the agent assigns the contract with the agreement of the principal to a third party.

When this legislation was introduced, many firms had to consider whether or not to change their sales and distribution network in the European Union because the new legislation gave much greater protection to agencies. As a result, some exporters replaced agencies with distributors and firms that continued with their agencies had to make sure that their agency agreements complied with the legislation.

Exporters considering appointing agents in the European Union should consult a lawyer about the details of the Commercial Agents Directive. If the agency agreements are not carefully drafted and agreed, exporters may not realise the extent of their liability in the event of termination of an agency agreement. In some cases, companies may consider setting up a distributorship rather than an agency.

Countries also differ in the extent to which businesses and consumers will resort to legal action. One of the consequences of the propensity to sue in the United States is that firms are advised to insure against the crippling damages and legal costs that can be awarded. This is never more true than when a company is selling products that have a high consequential risk. For example, manufacturers of crash helmets have been sued for large amounts of money by customers and relatives claiming that defects in the design and manufacture of helmets contributed to personal injury and deaths.

There is also the question of the single currency in the European Union. Those member states who have adopted the single currency find it easier to trade between these states and put countries outside the single currency agreement, such as the UK, at a disadvantage. Firms trading with countries outside the single currency still have to deal with the risks arising from fluctuating foreign exchange rates although one could argue that the single currency has had other detrimental effects on some economies.

ORGANISING MARKETING IN FOREIGN COUNTRIES

There are many ways in which firms market their goods internationally. Some do not require the exporter to have a direct presence in the foreign market at all. Other modes require the exporter to play an active role in setting up the sales and distribution channels in the foreign market. When firms sell in international markets with little or no presence in the markets, this is referred to as indirect exporting, where the products are sold in foreign markets without any special activity for this purpose being undertaken within the company. The export operations, including all the documentation, physical movement of goods and selling of the goods, are carried on by others. In contrast, direct exporting occurs where the firm undertakes the export task itself, builds up contacts, undertakes market research, handles documentation and transportation and develops marketing plans for the markets, either in conjunction with agents and distributors or through its own direct salespeople or sales subsidiary.

Figure 6.1   Market control and information versus resource commitment

Figure 6.1 illustrates the main options for operating overseas. Direct exporting gives a firm more control of the market and more market information compared with indirect exporting but more resources are committed. Export houses and buying houses are a low-risk method but do not have the potential of agents, distributors and sales subsidiaries to develop sales in a market.

EXPORT HOUSES

The functions performed by export houses vary but the most comprehensive role is where the export house buys from a firm and sells abroad on its own behalf. This has the following advantages for the firm:

- It does not have to sell in the international market.
- It is paid in the currency of the home market.

- It is not responsible for any of the export operation or for collecting payment from the buyers in the foreign market.

There are, however, disadvantages including the following:

- The lack of control over sales abroad, as export sales volume is entirely dependent on the performance of the export house.

- The image and reputation of the products are not within the control of the domestic firm.

- If the company sells on its own behalf at a later date, its efforts may be hindered by a product image and reputation not consistent with its marketing strategy at the time.

CONFIRMING HOUSE

When a foreign buyer places an order with a manufacturer, the manufacturer may want to protect itself from the possibility of non-payment by the foreign buyer. One way of doing this is for the exporter to agree terms with a confirming house, which will then guarantee payment to the UK manufacturer.

LOCAL BUYING OFFICES

Local buying offices are set up by organisations such as department store chains to buy goods from suppliers outside their home country. The buying office handles the export transaction with the exporter supplying the goods to the specification and price agreed. The manufacturer does not have any representation abroad and does not have any direct contact with the end-user. The advantage for the exporter is that sales to the consumer or the end-user are handled by the buying office and its parent company.

PIGGYBACK EXPORTING

As the term implies, this is an arrangement where a firm, the carrier, agrees to sell the products of another, the rider, through a sales network already built up by the carrier. The rider is often the smaller of the two parties. The agreement between the parties is usually that the carrier either sells the goods on a commission basis or acts as a distributor and buys the goods from the rider. Compared with export houses and buying offices, the rider may have more knowledge of the market depending on the relationship established with the carrier. Where this is the case, piggyback exporting has similarities with methods of direct exporting. For the rider, there are a number of advantages:

- The firm can use an existing sales network straight away, saving the time and costs of developing its own network.

- It is a comparatively low-risk method of selling because the investment in the international market is low.

- Being a low-risk, low-cost method of selling means that it is suitable for sales in markets where demand is small and which would otherwise not be worthwhile. Agents, distributors and a firm's own salesforce all require more time and money to develop than piggybacking.

- If the rider is not committed to exporting, piggybacking offers a way of developing international sales yet still leaves the rider free to concentrate on the domestic market.

The disadvantages are as follows:

- There may be difficulty in finding a suitable carrier.

- The rider's products may take second place to the carrier's product line, something which the rider may not find satisfactory.

- The rider does not have direct access to the market and does not build up a knowledge of customers in the market.

Piggyback exporting, like export houses and other indirect means of selling in foreign markets, has the advantages of

low risk and low cost for the new exporter but knowledge of
the market is restricted and sales growth is governed by the
activities of the carrier.

AGENTS

Agents represent an exporter directly in the market. Effectively,
they are the company abroad and, if the relationship between
the exporter and agents develops well, the exporter will have
much greater knowledge of the market compared with other
means of selling already discussed. In most situations, the
exporter can actively manage the agency, developing market
segments in a planned and progressive way. The exporter
should be able to work closely with the agency to formulate
marketing plans for the foreign market. To do this, the
exporter has to:

- be much more committed to exporting
- be prepared to invest the time and resources to find a
  good agent
- develop the relationship over a period of years.

Export agents have many roles in international markets.
Some agencies undertake all marketing activities on behalf of
the exporter while, at the other extreme, some agencies are
used simply as 'enquiry-finders' or 'lead generators' for their
principals. Such agents are often a small organisation, perhaps
run by one man with some administrative or secretarial
assistance. The agency's role is to pass on or generate enquiries
for the exporter, who will then visit the customer prospects,
usually with the agent as well. This restrictive service is
relatively cheap to provide and the commission paid to the
agent will be as low as perhaps 3% or 5% of the selling price.

DISTRIBUTORS

Whereas agencies operate on a commission basis and do not
take title to the goods, distributors buy the goods from the
exporter and make their money from their mark-up, that is,
the difference between the prices at which they buy and sell.

Generally speaking, distributors are larger organisations than agencies and are able to offer a wider range of functions.

COMPANY SALES REPRESENTATIVES

Using a company representative in a foreign market has several advantages:

- They have specialised knowledge of the company's products.
- They are familiar with the company's marketing strategy and are able to give feedback on customers and markets directly.
- Being a company employee, the sales representative is much more easily controlled and evaluated.

The disadvantages of using a sales representative are:

- Although international travel is nowadays much easier and arguably less expensive, there are limits to the time that a representative operating from the home market can spend abroad.
- If foreign languages are required, it may be difficult to recruit representatives who have the necessary language ability.
- They cannot be in the foreign market all the time and consequently the use of an agent or distributor may be preferred by foreign buyers and be seen as a sign of greater commitment to the market.

LOCAL SALES SUBSIDIARY

This is generally interpreted by foreign customers as a sign of greater commitment to the market. The decision facing the exporter is how to staff the sales office. Should the exporter use salespeople from the home market or should local salespeople be recruited? Locally recruited representatives have the advantage that they know the local culture, can speak the local language, if required, and may have previous experience in the industry. On the other hand, they lack knowledge of the exporter.

One of the advantages of the sales office is flexibility. The number of people employed can be expanded or reduced as sales rise or fall. Nevertheless, starting a sales subsidiary takes a considerable amount of time and resources and would usually not be the first mode of selling considered by an exporter.

Furthermore, where an exporter sets up sales subsidiaries in several countries staffed by local sales representatives, the exporter will have to consider how best to manage salesforces of different nationalities and cultures. The management of a salesforce in the domestic market is not likely to be an appropriate model for managing in other cultures such as in Japan and America:

- Firms in Japan provide more training and organisational culture-building activities than in America.

- The preferred way of motivating a Japanese salesforce is by fostering their commitment to the firm.

- Japanese sales representatives are more closely supervised, so a sales manager would be responsible for fewer representatives than in the United States.

- In the United States, it is much easier to set up a salesforce and financial rewards are a much more effective way of controlling the salesforce.

In the context of the discussion of culture earlier, these findings are not surprising but rather confirm the role of culture in shaping the beliefs and actions of individuals within a cultural grouping.

A summary of the characteristics, advantages and disadvantages of selling modes is given in Table 6.1.

Table 6.1 Export modes

Export mode	Characteristics	Advantages	Disadvantages
Indirect			
Export houses	There are a number of types of export but the most commonly understood is the organisation that buys from a firm and sells abroad on its own account	May handle all aspects of the export operation	Little market control or information. Limited sales
Confirming houses	Act on behalf of foreign buyers who pay them on a commission basis. The confirming house guarantees payment to the exporter on shipment of the goods	As above but also guarantees payment	As above
Buying houses	Acting on behalf of clients such as foreign department stores, buying houses purchase from domestic manufacturers	As above but the domestic manufacturer is approached by the buying house and need have no involvement in exporting other than supplying the order	Finding a suitable partner. The domestic company's product may take second priority. Growth may be impeded by existing arrangements
Agents	There are several types of agent: some will sell only one company's products; other agents will sell products from a number of companies, some of which may be competing. An agent does not take title to the goods, is usually a national of the country concerned and is paid on a commission basis	More market control and information than with the channels mentioned above. Permanent presence in the market. Costs of agency are related to sales	May sell more than one company's products. Agency agreements can be difficult and expensive to terminate
Distributors	The distributor takes title to the goods and therefore earns revenue from the mark-up on the product rather than the commission	Like the agent, knows the local market. Able to provide after-sales service. More control of the market	Costs of termination are high should exporter's market development plans require new channels

Export mode	Characteristics	Advantages	Disadvantages
Direct			
Direct selling	Sales representatives operating from the home country may be used in foreign sales territories	Detailed knowledge of the company and its products. High level of market control and information	Suffers from a lack of market knowledge, increased travelling time and, depending on the country, language problems
Local sales offices	These may be staffed by representatives either from the home market or from the foreign market	Perceived as a commitment to the market. Easier for local companies to deal with the exporter. Flexible and can accommodate growth	Problem of choosing appropriate personnel for the sales force. Domestic reps may be reluctant to move overseas; local reps have less company knowledge but more country/market know-how

FOREIGN MARKETING RELATIONSHIPS

Exporter–importer relationships are dynamic. Some relationships endure while others flourish, decline and die. This is partly because the exporter wants to develop markets and discards the first intermediary used, often indirect intermediaries, as the market develops. Exporters increasingly used direct means of access to the marketplace over time. Agents particularly are used so that closer contact can be established and maintained with customers abroad. Table 6.2 shows possible reasons for change from the perspective of those exporting to a specific country.

The patterns of relationships built up during foreign market entry and development are complex although most exporters are willing to use a range of different forms as business circumstances change and markets develop and mature. Most exporters use around four types of sales organisation for exporting, ranging from buyers based in the home market through to sales subsidiaries. Not only are companies prepared to use several forms of selling in foreign markets but they will also use more than one means of selling in a market where necessary.

Table 6.2 Changes in exporter–distributor relationships

Source of change		Response to change
1. Changes in sales	Poor sales	The distributorship split
	Good sales	Changed role for the distributor
		Distributor agreement terminated and other arrangements for sales were made
2. Changes in the status of the exporter	Exporter closed	Relationship ended
	Ownership of the exporter changed	Country becomes a lower market priority
		Rationalisation of international marketing
		Exporter and foreign distributor come under common ownership
3. Changes in the environment	Exchange rate became unfavourable	Exports to country stop
	Market dies	Exports to country stop
		New products sold through corporate sales network in country

If it is the case that exporters may work with several sales intermediaries, it is also true that agents and distributors frequently work for more than one exporter. Given this fact, the management of the exporter–intermediary relationship is especially important because if the exporter does not work effectively with the intermediary, the intermediary will put more effort into working with the other exporters it has links with.

Finally, it should be noted that sales subsidiaries set up by exporters also take on agents. The reasons that sales subsidiaries hold a number of agencies on behalf of other manufacturers is that this spreads the costs of operating the subsidiary over a wider product range and careful selection of agencies can improve the attractiveness of the subsidiary's main product.

THE MANAGEMENT OF EXPORTER–AGENCY/ DISTRIBUTOR RELATIONSHIPS

Evidence and experience show that more than half of export marketing ventures fail because the wrong distributor was selected. Usually the reasons for this are that the distributor company had not the technical experience claimed, had exaggerated its influence with buyers, was poorly located, and was not prepared to commit itself to the exporter's products. Getting it right at the beginning is essential. This confirms the importance of agency/distributor relationships and underlines the fact that many firms do not manage these relationships well. This is supported by many studies that have found that firms cited establishing sales and distribution networks in foreign markets as a problem. How then do exporters manage these relationships effectively?

SELECTING AGENTS/DISTRIBUTORS

The sources most frequently used to identify potential distributors are personal visits to search the territory but government sources through the British Overseas Trade Board are also used, as are colleagues, customer recommendations and trade fairs. Also, a number of firms find that their source for identifying overseas distributors is often an unsolicited contact by distributors.

Most exporters use similar criteria when selecting their agents/distributors. The criteria can be split into three categories:

- sales and market factors
- product and service factors
- risk and uncertainty factors.

The most frequently used criteria are market and customer knowledge and customer contacts, not carrying competitors' products, enthusiasm for the contract and hunger to succeed. These factors emphasise the basic reason for choosing foreign distributors, which is to obtain effective market representation. It is essential for the success of the exporter that the distributor has these characteristics. Exporters clearly prefer to have a distributor concentrate on their own products rather than divide their time between competing products. It would seem, at least for some of the firms, that it is more important to have distributors who are enthusiastic and have good knowledge of the market than to have generally good track records and good financial standing. The majority of firms draw up a shortlist of potential distributors and interview them in their own country, which underlines the importance in the selection process of personal contact in market surroundings.

MOTIVATION

An exporter needs to understand what will motivate its intermediaries abroad. With the caveat that different motivations may apply across different countries, exporters need to look carefully at each market. Perhaps most important is the need to maintain effective exporter/distributor communication. These include keeping the distributor up to date and maintaining regular personal contact.

Generally, the most important criteria in managing the exporter–agency relationship are:

- high/consistent product quality
- competitive prices
- suppliers' fairness and trustworthiness
- an ability to keep his/her promises.

Clearly, fairness, trust and keeping promises are important issues in working with and motivating an agent/distributor.

EVALUATION

Nearly all the firms evaluate their distributors, most on an annual basis. Criteria and standards vary but most exporters employ a wide range of criteria and, not surprisingly, achieving sales is the most frequently used evaluation measure. Sales volume, sales value and new business are commonly applied. In some situations criteria include the quality of the distributor's market feedback, customer services and selling/ marketing inputs. Comparison against past performance is an often-used approach.

The conclusions to be drawn about the management of exporter–agent/distributor relationships is that good personal contact and joint decision-making with the channel members have a positive bearing on export performance. The rationale for this must be sought in the fact that increasing personal contact will lead the firm to a better understanding of customers' and channel members' needs and behaviour. Improved target market selection, adaptation of marketing policy and better relations with channel members – including qualified joint decision-making – are the natural consequences which affect performance positively. The reason for better performance may be attributed to better decision quality and larger commitment from both parties. Good personal contact with the market and a close relationship with channel members further enhance the exporter's capability for careful planning and the control of sales in export markets.

There is a great deal of debate in the academic literature about exactly how firms increase their international activities, of which increasing the capacity to sell is one dimension. The competing explanations of internationalisation emphasise different aspects of firm behaviour and the environment. Internationalisation is not necessarily a formal rational process, although, as already identified, there is much support for the view that firms who assess international markets and plan their market entry and development improve their chances of success.

The discussion of the forms of organisation in this chapter has emphasised that, when firms are choosing sales intermediaries, there is a trade-off between the control of marketing activities and access to market information required versus the resources committed to that market. The decision to use a particular type of sales intermediary is partly based on the firm's assessment of these factors. Apart from this, the choice of sales intermediary is influenced by:

- the firm's own international marketing strategy;

- the structure of the exporter's industry, which may place constraints on the types of selling organisation used; for example, if competitors providing after-sales service is important, direct forms of export are more likely to be used;

- the operating environment of the firm abroad; for example, selling in Japan usually means working with an intermediary in the first instance.

PRICING

Compared with selling in the home market, selling in foreign markets entails a number of additional activities and costs that increase prices. This is sometimes referred to as price escalation and the effect on the final price of some of these factors is shown in Table 6.3. In the example, there are additional shipping costs and tariffs in the foreign market but otherwise both channels are similar. Nevertheless, the final price is 68% higher in the foreign market. If more intermediaries are used, the price will increase even more.

Exporters, however, do have a choice of how they calculate the costs of manufacture of the goods exported. They may take a view that the fixed costs of manufacturing will not be spread evenly across all production, regardless of its destination, but attributed only to production for the home market. The decision could be to attribute only the variable costs of production to the product destined for export markets. This means a lower price abroad.

Selling at low prices in a market may, however, lead to charges of dumping and governments may put an additional

Table 6.3   Price escalation

	Domestic market (£)	Foreign market (£)
Manufacturer's price	10.00	10.00
Shipping costs		4.00
Landed cost		14.00
Tariff (20%)		2.80
Distributor's cost	10.00	16.80
Distributor's margin (33⅓% on cost)	3.33	5.60
Retailer's cost	13.33	22.40
Retailer's margin (40% on cost)	5.33	8.96
Retail price	18.66	31.36
Price escalation (%)		+68%

tariff on the goods to raise the price, but anti-dumping charges are fraught with problems because it is difficult to establish exactly what costs should be attributed to exported products. It is precisely this problem of determining costs that allows some governments to use anti-dumping charges as a barrier to trade. They unfairly protect local industry by imposing a levy when it is not warranted, in effect protecting inefficient home market manufacturers from genuinely competitive foreign competition.

An important aspect of pricing in international markets is how the price is quoted. Should it be a fully delivered price, that is, delivery duty paid, where the exporter quotes for delivery to the customer's premises and agrees to do all that is necessary, such as preparing the documentation, arranging insurance, shipping the goods, paying any tariffs and clearing customs? Alternatively, the exporter might make the goods available at its own premises and quote an ex-works price which only includes the cost of manufacture. The customer bears all the costs and takes responsibility for transporting the consignment.

In international trade, there is an internationally agreed set of terms of trade called Incoterms which specify the duties and obligations of the exporter and importer when using an Incoterm such as ex-works (EXW) or delivery duty paid (DDP). Incoterms drafted by the International Chamber of Commerce (ICC) were last revised in 1990. Hence they are currently known as Incoterms (1990) and are a reference point in a court of law in the event of a dispute.

Another aspect of pricing is the cost and provision of credit. Exporters can arrange for their credit arrangements to be handled by other organisations, but many firms make their own arrangements for credit assessment and provision. It is important that credit references are taken out on customers initially and on a continuing basis. References can be taken out through credit-checking agencies based in the exporter's home country, such as Dun & Bradstreet or Infocheck, or it may be cheaper to go direct to foreign-based agencies which provide services across a number of countries. Example of these are:

- Sereco, based in Egypt, covering most of the Middle East
- Harlow, based in the USA, covering all of North America and Canada
- the Maypole, based in Bangladesh, which covers a very large area including the Far East and Africa.

In offering credit, the exporter has to balance the provisions of attractive, cheap, long-term credit to gain more orders against short-term and expensive credit which may lead to a loss of orders. To find the ideal balance, a firm should develop its own credit policy by deciding on such questions as:

- What percentage of total assets should be represented by debtors?
- What will be the range of credit terms on offer?
- How will the creditworthiness of new customers be assessed?
- How will the company deal with slow payment and default?

Putting together tailor-made credit packages depends upon knowledge of the customer. The kinds of information sought should include the taking of credit references, credit terms desired and detailed information about the customer, possibly given through the use of a formal credit application. Clearly, the firm should have a clear idea of the cost of credit, which is determined by:

- the quantity of credit sales
- the average credit period
- the opportunity cost of capital.

A firm's credit policy should have a monitoring system to help to identify problems with customers and with the functioning of the policy within the firm's financial structure. For example, monitoring the ratio of credit sales to total sales enables the firm to see and assess changes in its risk exposure. The ratio of bad debts to total credit sales provides a view of how well the firm is managing the approval of credit applications and the collection of credit.

SUMMARY

Selling in international markets presents new challenges for the firm selling abroad for the first time. The various facets of the international marketing environment directly affect the selling activities of firms. Busy managers need to understand, for example, the role of culture in shaping diverse negotiating styles and the impact of legislation on the selection and management of agents and distributors.

Much of the research on successful exporting supports the view that planning pays. If the firm assesses a market it is interested in and plans how it is going to enter and develop that market, it will increase its chances of success.

Research on the management of agents and distributors underlines the unstable nature of some relationships and the necessity carefully to select agents and distributors. Those managers who consciously build close relationships with their agents and distributors will usually have more success in foreign markets.

Besides the above, there are many additional issues which the new exporter has to master. These include dealing with export documentation, selecting appropriate Incoterms and setting prices. Some firms may see these issues as a barrier to success but, given the commitment of management, there is no reason why a firm should not sell successfully in international markets.

FINAL WORD

In setting out to write this book, the author was determined to bring to the attention of the non-professional marketer as many of the principal features of marketing that size and space available in the book would allow. In doing so, he is conscious of the fact that this condensation does not permit the inclusion of many academic references to support the uncontested dogma nor the wealth of practical examples to back up the theory. Nevertheless the economy of space has forced a certain brevity and clarity of language, which in turn has made the message short and sharp!

Marketing controls and guides your business activities and the principles and practices, which have been established and refined over the years by the professionals involved in this field, have a relevance to and may be utilised by any business, regardless of size. It does not require the services of a professional marketer to put into practice the marketing theory and the planning principles outlined in this book. If you know your business, then the practical implementation of marketing to suit the requirements of your business is an important, but very short, step.

There are, of course, many facets to the individual aspects of marketing, which require a practical application. The use of marketing research to gather customer information is a case in point. The diversity of business makes it well-nigh impossible to produce a stylised research programme or questionnaire to cover all possibilities. However, it is possible with a degree of thought and application to produce research that will suit your purposes in line with the marketing theory with which you have been presented. This book should act as a trigger for such thoughts.

This book is one of a number in the 'Busy Manager' series and will be followed by dedicated books, in a similar style, on each of the principal components of business. In the true traditions of marketing, we would be most grateful for feedback or any comment you may have on this book to allow us to maintain and improve the quality of the product. Happy and successful marketing to you all!

INDEX

Lightning Source UK Ltd
Milton Keynes UK
14 January 2010

148579UK00001B/54/P